Contents

Preface

This book has been written with three objectives: first, to present the findings of a survey investigation conducted in 1972; second, to advocate, develop, refine and illustrate the use of the class imagery concept in the study of stratification; and third, to interpret certain currents of change in contemporary British society. Had we settled for any one of these aims there would have been fewer loose ends in the book's arguments, and perhaps it attempts too much. But if sociology is to be something more than just another academic pastime, we feel that it must attempt to put it all together, meaning that the subject must relate its theoretical concerns and research equipment to the analysis of real social issues and events. The fit is inevitably ragged—theories can rarely be operationalised without losing some of their conceptual elegance and the data gleaned from any research project, however rigorously executed, can never be more than a small sample of all the information relevant to an issue such as how the class structure is changing.

Remaining in the realm of theory makes coherence easier to achieve, just as limiting discussion to hypotheses that can be rigorously tested makes it easier to draw definite conclusions. Sociologists can feel safe in these retreats, but the longer they remain so enclosed the less their subject can say about society. This book comes out of these corners and thereby, we hope, says something that will be of interest beyond the côterie of professional colleagues, for we feel that the substantive issues examined are important and deserve public discussion. We are sure that many of our conclusions about the fragmentary class structure will be challenged. Indeed, we hope that the class images we have identified will be refined and possibly replaced by yet more fruitful concepts and that future researchers will re-examine and re-interpret topics such as the growth of white-collar trade unionism. No one ever completely closes an argument in any science, sociology included.

There are four authors of this book but many other individuals have also assisted in its production. Needless to say, the latter bear no responsibility for the volume's shortcomings. We acknowledge the help received at various stages from our colleagues at Liverpool University: Professor J. B. Mays, K. G. Pickett, and K. Margerison. The fieldwork was completed with the assistance of E. Diaper, N. Swift, D. Jones, S. Gee, E. Bird, C. E. Robertson, and J. Walker. Our thanks are also due to the secretarial staff of the Sociology Department at the University for the typing of the manuscript. Last but by no means least, we acknowledge the support of the Social Science Research Council who financed the fieldwork upon which this book is based.

The Fragmentary Class Structure

K. Roberts   F. G. Cook   S. C. Clark
Elizabeth Semeonoff

HEINEMANN · LONDON

London Edinburgh Melbourne Auckland Toronto
Hong Kong Singapore Kuala Lumpur New Delhi
Nairobi Johannesburg Lusaka Ibadan
Kingston

ISBN 0 435 82765 0
Paperback ISBN 0 82766 9
© Roberts, Cook, Clark and Semeonoff 1977
First published 1977

Published by Heinemann Educational Books Ltd
48 Charles Street, London W1X 8AH
Printed in Great Britain by Butler & Tanner Ltd
Frome and London

1. Introduction

Inequality has long been one of sociology's big issues. Prominent figures in the discipline's history have addressed the problem of how societies could be most usefully analysed to uncover the sources and consequences of inequality and, long before the term sociology was coined, many of history's most perceptive thinkers had already attempted explanations, justifications and criticisms of the persistence of inequalities. Against this backcloth the endeavours of any contemporary sociologist grappling with the problem of social class easily fall prey to charges of pretension. The sociologist's research techniques are puny in relation to the issues at stake and their use often seems a poor pretext for qualifying oneself to exchange ideas with the eminent.

One strategy guaranteed to maintain an air of modesty is for the sociologist to disclaim interest in the big issues such as the sources of inequality and to rest content with one small aspect of the topic such as describing the distribution of occupational incomes. But the problem about splintering the subject of class is that it opens itself to the charge of trivialising the topic. Successive investigations, each cornering some special issue, fail to produce results which add up to a resolution of more fundamental questions about the overall shape and determinants of a system of stratification.

We hope to skate between these pitfalls. In our view, the issues addressed, which concern changes in patterns of class division amongst the working population in contemporary society, are anything but trivial—and by developing and using the concept of class imagery we hope to genuinely illuminate these issues.

Images of class

Sociologists have long appreciated that individuals are able and willing to name the social classes to which they belong. Hence it has been common for investigators to ask 'Which class do you belong to?' and in Britain, alongside other western countries, it has been found that most responses employ some derivative of the terms 'working' or 'middle class'. Further probing, it has been discovered, can solicit more sophisticated impressions of where individuals feel they stand in the social hierarchy, so in the nineteen-thirties, Warner and his colleagues embarked upon a series of investigations to discover how members of various communities ranked each other and with whom they associated as equals and consequently distinguished six classes in American society.[1]

The problem with these straightforward approaches is that they fail to do justice to their subject. Phrases such as working and middle class mean different things to different people, while individuals' views and feelings about their positions in the class structure cannot be properly condensed into a single measure of how they rank each other along a linear scale. Comprehensively examining subjective aspects of stratification also requires exploring, for example, whether existing class differences are felt to be fair or unjust and whether individuals' attitudes towards members of other classes are emulative or antagonistic. In recent years, therefore, attempts have been made to probe behind the labels used in identifying their positions, to discover comprehensively the characteristics individuals believe members of their own classes share and the ways in which they define the relationships between their own and other classes. The products of these endeavours have been variously termed configurations, class ideologies, images of society and meaning systems. For consistency we will talk about images of class and a purpose of this book is to recommend their exploration.

Sociologists are concerned with images of class partly because they supply otherwise missing colourful detail and this may be considered of intrinsic interest. A more important reason, however, is that on account of its detail this information can enable connections between subjective and objective aspects of stratification to be established. All serious students of stratification have recognised that there are both objective and subjective aspects to this phenomenon. By this is meant that in all societies one finds inequalities of income, wealth, educational opportunities and so on, which have an objective existence in so far as investigators can make statements about their proportions without reference to the ideas, beliefs or feelings of the members of the society concerned. The likelihood, however, is that the members of a society will have ideas about the system of inequality amidst which they live. They may regard themselves as working class or middle class, as fairly or under-privileged, and such aspects of stratification are subjective in that an investigator can gather information about them only by somehow gaining access to the contents of the minds of the persons involved.

All the main issues concerning social class involve exploring the inter-connections between objective and subjective phenomena. For analytical purposes, it is certainly possible to compartmentalise their investigation. It is possible, for example, to simply collect information about the distribution of income and wealth. However, the very use of a term such as class implies something more than that income, wealth and other resources are unevenly distributed. As others have previously observed, differences of occupation, income, education and suchlike only acquire a hierarchical character and thereby become bases for stratification in so far as individuals evaluate these differences and rank each other accordingly. In the absence of such subjective processes, the concept of social class would be redundant and answering questions about the shape of a society's class structure necessarily involves exploring the inter-connections between its objective and subjective aspects.

In accomplishing this a problem arises from the fact that there may be no simple causal link between the objective and subjective aspects of stratification. Indeed, there is often a perplexing lack of fit between men's ideas about the schemes of inequality surrounding them and the dimensions of inequality apparent to an external observer. For example, in their study of an economically depressed district in Nottingham, Coates and Silburn[2] show that individuals living on extremely low incomes in relation to standards prevailing throughout society-at-large can nevertheless feel 'not too badly off'.

A method of analysis favoured by many European sociologists, influenced by the Marxian tradition though not necessarily Marxists, has attached primacy to objective aspects of stratification in the sense that attention has been focused upon the relations of production, authority relationships or the distribution of income and subjective manifestations of stratification have been examined in relation to the structures thus revealed. So in exploring subjective aspects of stratification, investigators have used terms such as true and false, or necessary and contingent class consciousness. They have sought to discover whether individuals are aware of the objective inequalities surrounding them and, if not, to identify the factors that distort individuals' perceptions.

Up to a point this can be a useful procedure but there are a number of weaknesses. To begin with, the treatment of subjective aspects of stratification is unlikely to be adequate. Assessing subjective phenomena in terms of how closely they reflect certain independently established objective facts can ride roughshod over individuals' authentic ideas and feelings. Whilst individuals' ideas may sometimes be invalid, they are nevertheless likely to have real consequences and hence the importance of discovering what individuals really feel and think.

Furthermore, it is mistaken to presume that an observer, even a sociologist, is able to identify *the* objective features of any situation. In recent years there has been much discussion of the problem of objectivity in the social sciences and this is hardly the place to dwell at length on the general issues involved. Suffice it to say that many-sided but equally objective descriptions are possible of all areas of social life. The appearance of reality depends upon the perspective from which it is approached and no human mind, including the sociologist's, simply absorbs the imprint of pure reality. If we take a simple aspect of stratification such as inequality of income, we can see that it is possible to categorise the distribution in various ways; along a linear scale according to amount, according to source, or according to the life-styles that different levels of income will support. The one certainty is that to treat the subject we must adopt some method of categorisation otherwise we are unable to handle the evidence. What we cannot do is to assume that one preferred method of categorisation enjoys a unique affinity with objective reality.

Studies of the class structure need to remain sensitive to its alternative appearances and the class imagery concept meets this criterion. Exploring images of class does not assume that perfect reflections of the systems of inequality amidst which individuals live will be disclosed. The underlying assumption is rather that people will see their society not as would an external and impartial observer, but from various ego-centric positions, resulting in the same social reality creating different images amongst its component publics. Exploring class images can help explain how given systems of inequality generate various types of subjective response. A repeated though contested theme in studies of class imagery has been that how individuals perceive the class structure depends not so much upon the shape of the macro-scheme of inequality, but upon the social relationships in which they are immediately involved. Elizabeth Bott[3] initially expounded this theme, arguing that class ideologies result from individuals internalising the norms of the primary groups to which they belong, reducing them to a common denominator, and projecting these norms onto society-at-large.

Bott juxtaposed power model and prestige ideologies. In the power model, society is seen as divided into 'us', usually the working class, and 'them' with conflicting interests. Individuals subscribing to this type of ideology display no desire to become individually mobile, but aspire to a better deal for their class as a whole, regarding it as lacking power but not prestige. Bott argues that this type of ideology tends to arise amongst working class communities with closed social networks, meaning where there is little geographical and social mobility—and where family, neighbourhood and workplace relationships are superimposed upon each other. This type of fraternal local milieu, it is alleged, stimulates an us–them image of the wider society. Against this power model Bott juxtaposes a prestige hierarchy type of imagery, individuals subscribing to which are conscious essentially of variations in prestige, seeing themselves as somewhere in the middle of the hierarchy and wanting to better their positions. Bott argues that prestige imagery is formed as a projection of the norms associated with the more open types of social network characteristic of the middle classes.

This, however, is only one view about how class images are generated. Parkin[4] and Ossowski[5] prefer to emphasise the ideological functions of meanings systems which they relate to the interests of groups located at different levels in the social hierarchy and suggest that propagating appropriate images of society is a strategy that dominant classes can use to legitimise and thereby consolidate their positions. Exactly how various forms of class imagery arise is currently open to dispute and there have been contributions to the debate other than those mentioned above. The point being made here, however, is that the concept of class imagery is sufficiently sensitive to enable the processes through which subjective aspects of stratification arise to be investigated and disputed.

At the same time, identifying class images can help explain how objective features of the class structure are sustained. Men's ideas may be influenced by but, at the same time, can help to shape the objectively measurable environments that they inhabit. How individuals react to any given system of inequality will depend not simply upon its contours as apparent to an independent observer, but upon how the individuals themselves perceive and evaluate the system. Any individual's behaviour in economic, political and other spheres of life can be illuminated by discovering how he regards his predicament. Systems of inequality are not part of any natural order, but are constructed, maintained and changed by the collective actions of individuals. Setting individuals' orientations towards action in the context of their images of the class structure, therefore, can help to explain how systems of inequality are both sustained and changed. Studying class images promises to do more than add a touch of colour to our knowledge about subjective aspects of stratification.

It allows both sides of the interplay between stratification's subjective and objective aspects to be examined, and it is within this interplay that the answers are to be found to many key questions concerning the shape of the class structure.

Searching for the class images is not entirely uncontroversial and can evoke a number of objections. Firstly it can be argued that probing for class images may put ideas into respondents' heads and words into their mouths. Views on class are notoriously difficult to probe without investigators 'leading' their respondents. Merely asking people to name the classes they belong to runs the risk of producing spontaneous verbal nonsense and if this is so, then seeking more complex images of the class structure is even more suspect. Secondly it can be argued that seeking 'images' assumes that people's ideas about class possess a logical consistency that may not actually be present. Individuals may possess a variety of discrete and, if juxtaposed, contradictory views and if this is so, then soliciting 'comprehensive' images of the class structure may distort the subjective realities of stratification. The replies to these objections are as follows. As far as the charge of putting words into people's mouths is concerned, the unanimous experience of sociologists who have studied subjective aspects of stratification in modern western societies is that few people need to be pushed into talking about class. Ideas flow freely, making it unlikely that individuals' expressions are merely conjured up by the mechanics of the research situation. If the answers individuals gave to questions about class were random vocalisations offered purely to satisfy the probing investigator, one would not expect the information so obtained to be meaningfully related to other data, but as we shall see, this is emphatically not the case. The danger that an investigator's tools will contaminate the information he collects is present in all types of research, but there is no *prima facie* case for treating this as a special objection to the class imagery concept.

As regards the charge that the concept may 'round out' individuals' views and make them appear more consistent than they really are, as we shall show, this is not in fact a potential source of error. In studying class imagery, as in examining other areas of social life, it is useful to employ ideal-types which are explicitly recognised as unrealistically rational constructs. However, provided the difference between such a construct and the real world is appreciated, no gross distortion need occur.

Whatever its potential might be, it must be admitted that the study of class imagery remains in its infancy in the sense, for example, that there are no typologies whose utility has been convincingly demonstrated. Typologies have been proposed, but never with wholly convincing claims to plausibility. Existing typologies divide rather neatly into two groups; those that are theoretically derived and supported by a very limited amount of evidence, and those based firmly upon survey research but whose relevance beyond the populations studied remains unclear.

Elizabeth Bott advanced the hypothesis, already introduced above, that class ideologies are directly responsive to the primary social relationships in which individuals are immediately involved and she distinguished situations conducive to power model and prestige hierarchy ideologies. Reasoning along essentially similar lines, David Lockwood has distinguished three types of working class milieux respectively nurturing proletarian, deferential and pecuniary images of society.[6] Other theoretically derived typologies, however, treat class images as reflecting different class interests rather than the social relationships by which individuals are directly surrounded. Ossowski's work falls under this heading and a comparable typology has been developed by Frank Parkin.[7] He distinguishes, firstly, dominant meaning systems emanating from superordinate classes and justifying the existing social order. Secondly, he recognises accommodative meaning systems in which the dominant ideology is negotiated to fit the realities of lower class life so that existing inequalities may be accepted, but fatalistically rather than enthusiastically. Thirdly, he sketches a radical meaning system which explicitly challenges the necessity and justice of existing inequalities. The resemblance of these hypothesised meaning systems to real social phenomena, however, remains untested and likewise, Bott's typology was based upon the results of interviews with only twenty London families.

A second group of typologies have been constructed in an *ad hoc* manner from data supplied by their authors' survey investigations. A five-fold typology emerged from the 146 interviews that Davies conducted amongst an occupationally heterogeneous sample in Melbourne.[8] Davies distinguished a group of respondents conscious of only the faintest class divisions, another that regarded everyone as middle class but recognised layers within this category, another that was conscious of an intricate prestige hierarchy with many fine and subtle distinctions, another that saw society structured like a pyramid with classes becoming larger as the scale was descended, and a final group that divided the population into a large working class and a smaller upper group. Hiller's research,[9] also conducted in Australia, led to the construction of an even more complex eight-fold typology. In these empirically based schemes, some overlap with the forms of class imagery defined in the theoretically derived typologies can be found, but there is no close fit. Of course, the validity of the empirically based schemes could be limited to the populations studied. At the same time, however, the ability of theoretically derived types to clarify actual systems of stratification must be regarded as unproven.

Despite leaving many uncertainties, the existing literature on class imagery offers a foundation upon which further research can build. Firstly, it enables us to recognise the dimensions along which class images are likely to vary. The empirical studies show that images can vary according to the number of classes recognised; according to the perceived shape of the hierarchy—whether it is pyramidal or diamond-shaped, for example; according to the factors regarded as determining individuals' class positions such as occupation and income; according to whether whatever classes are recognised are regarded as co-existing in harmony or in conflict; according to whether or not social mobility is seen as desirable and possible; according to whether the system of inequality is felt to be just; and finally, according to whether or not individuals feel that it can be subjected to change. Secondly, the theoretical literature offers a number of hypotheses concerning the sources and consequences of different class images, and our research attempts to carry the study of class imagery forward from these foundations.

Social class and social change

We intend to clarify the sources, consequences and types of class imagery that occur amongst the working population in a modern industrial society, and in the course of doing so we hope to prove that the investigation of class imagery can be fruitful by addressing a set of inter-related questions about the effects of broader social changes upon the class structure. The purpose of this book, therefore, is not merely to make a conceptual point, that class imagery constitutes a sensible area for sociological enquiry. Our intention is rather to explore class images in order to shed light on more familiar issues.

Our arguments concern the implications of contemporary currents of occupational, economic, urban and educational change. To begin with, there is the white/blue collar or middle/working class cleavage. Both sociologists and laymen frequently juxtapose the working and middle classes, but to what extent do these concepts still tap a real division of interest and ideology? Are there any distinctly working class values? If so, is it the case, as is often supposed, that individual ambition is a specifically middle class quality, whilst working class values emphasise collective loyalties and consequently exclude a quest for individual betterment, including through education?

Some writers have suggested that this traditionally recognised schism is becoming less severe, the embourgeoisement thesis—maintaining that former sections of the working class are being assimilated into the middle classes—being one prominent example. It is certainly beyond argument that the circumstances of the manual strata are changing. Rising wage levels and the spread of employment amongst wives have pushed standards of living well above the subsistence levels of pre-war years. School-leavers entering working class occupations today have received as many years schooling as middle class youngsters obtained in the days when access to secondary education was ordinarily by payment. The welfare state has transformed many former privileges of the few including paid holidays, retirement pensions, health and legal services, and income maintenance during periods of sickness and unemployment into rights of citizenship. In urban areas there has been a massive resettlement of working class families from older 'slum' districts to modern flats and housing estates, some owned and managed by local authorities, others owner-occupied. Throughout all these developments, however, one school of thought has resisted notions of the manual worker being assimilated into the middle classes and insisted upon the ability of working class values to survive improvements in material circumstances. Others have argued that while not becoming bourgeois, traditional working class values and life-styles are being replaced by a new privatised, instrumentally oriented and commodity-conscious working class culture. Meanwhile, amidst the debate surrounding the embourgeoisement thesis and its alternatives, Marxist commentators have continued to argue that the working class remains liable to coalesce into a radical and solidaristic class for itself. Any current lack of revolutionary ardour has been attributed to an ideological hegemony temporarily maintained by superordinate strata. But is this the major obstacle to revolutionary solidarity? Exactly what is the state of the contemporary working class and what are the directions of change?

The position of the white-collar worker in the class structure has recently been exciting as much comment as the state of the working class. The proportion of white-collar employees in the working population is increasing and, in Britain, it is expected that, by the end of the century, the manual strata will be outnumbered. This has already happened in America. Hence the claim that advanced industrial societies are becoming increasingly middle class is not without some foundation. But what type of middle class is growing? Commentators have agreed that the middle class is changing. A generation ago, it was conventional to treat self-employed business men and professional people as archetypal middle class figures. Middle class values have traditionally emphasised the virtues of individual enterprise, the security that accompanies the possession of private property and the desirability of conserving one's assets along with the social arrangements that made their accumulation possible. Will the growth of the white-collar sector lead to the spread of these traditional middle class values or is a new middle class being shaped and, if so, what values will it nurture?

We intend to consider the implications of the growth of large-scale corporations, and the creation of salaried armies of clerks and administrators. Is the product, as some writers have claimed, an acquiescent middle mass of organisation men? Or does the development of white-collar trade unionism indicate that former sections of the middle class are being proletarianised? According to one school of thought, the work situations, income levels and career prospects of many white-collar employees now differ little from those of the manual working class and the socio-political values of the new white-collar proletariat are expected to fall into line. Another development requiring exploration concerns the growth of higher education and a professionally qualified section of the middle class. Some writers have attributed distinctly radical tendencies to this section of the population. Since the nineteen-sixties the student radical has been a familiar creature, but to what extent and in what shape is his radicalism liable to survive his student days?

Across all these more specific questions an underlying theme involves identifying cut-off points where significant divisions occur. Conventionally the middle/working class schism has been taken as a major point of cleavage. Current trends, however, could be blurring this divide and opening new rifts.

The above issues are not new. Each has been the subject of considerable previous research and argument. Our intention, however, is not merely to review the debates but to carry them forward by reconsidering the issues in the light of fresh evidence from our own and other recent enquiries that clarify the images of class existing amongst different sections of the population.

The topics that we will consider by no means amount to a comprehensive examination of the class structure. For instance, we have little to say about the problems of poverty and powerlessness that particularly beset economically inactive sections of the population. Nor are the positions of élite groups, the extremely rich and powerful, examined in any depth. These issues are excluded not because they are unimportant and certainly not because they lie outside the terms of a study of social class. It is simply that social class is a big subject and this book focuses upon particular problem areas. Our approach is not strictly comparative. The focus is on Britain. The issues, however, are relevant in other modern societies and we hope, therefore, to contribute towards understanding some of the forms of stratification that are taking shape throughout the industrial world.

While not exhausting the subject of social class, the above issues are anything but trivial. The bulk of the population consists of workers and their families and their circumstances cannot be dismissed as of negligible importance. Numbers apart, however, patterns of class division amongst the working population have a general socio-political relevance. Party political loyalties and alignments in the industrial arena tend to follow the class divisions under discussion. Any changes in this social class infra-structure, therefore, deserve more than purely academic interest.

Research methods

Addressing all the questions surveyed above in a single investigation may appear excessively ambitious. In fact the breadth is parsimonious on account of the evidence required to explore the different issues overlapping to a considerable extent. Assessing what is happening to affluent manual employees, routine office workers and other specific groups, at some stage always requires their comparison with others and the value of many previous enquiries has been limited because characteristics of groups other than the one being principally examined have been tentatively inferred rather than systematically investigated.

Our research consists of interviews during 1972 with 474 economically active males from a sample selected at random from the electoral registers covering the adjacent Woolton and Allerton districts of Liverpool. The fieldwork was conducted in a particular area but the investigation was not designed as a 'locality study'. We set out with the intention of studying neither a 'community' nor the overall way of life of the inhabitants in a particular district. We conducted the research in a specific area rather than working with a regional or national sample for reasons of convenience and cost, and because this enabled local influences, upon life-styles for example, to be held constant in the research design. The Woolton/Allerton area was selected because census data indicated that it contained the types of subjects required to address the problems with which the enquiry was concerned. Woolton and Allerton house an occupationally heterogeneous population with similar numbers in white-collar and manual jobs, distributed throughout the Registrar General's social classes. The area is situated on Liverpool's suburban fringe with predominantly owner-occupied accommodation representing a wide range of price-brackets but also containing a large, modern council estate. We expected that the population at both extremes of the socio-economic hierarchy would be represented thinly, if at all, in our sample. The area is not part of any 'stockbroker belt' nor is it a run-down, inner-city district. However, it contained subjects in the variety of circumstances we needed to locate and it is the type of area in which the bulk of the working population is increasingly living.

Respondents were selected by a simple random sample of male names from the electoral register. Following an introductory letter an interviewer called and, in cases where the person was contacted, confirmed that the individual was male and established whether he was economically active, meaning either working or available for employment. Amongst the economically active males identified, a response rate of 69 per cent was achieved. Non-response occurred mainly where it proved impossible to arrange a mutually convenient time for the interview which was scheduled to last for at least an hour-and-a-half and, in many cases, ran for much longer. There were a few outright refusals but, in general, as field-workers invariably find, once people heard about the survey they were mostly keen to take part. Indeed, when our introductory letters were re-addressed and forwarded to individuals who had left the district, we received replies from many parts of Britain from would-be respondents expressing interest in the enquiry and wondering if their participation could be arranged.

The sample was restricted to the economically active because our interest lay in stratification amongst the working population, and, confined to males because the division of labour between the sexes was not an issue with which we were concerned and, by excluding women, we were able to hold the gender variable constant in the research design. The changing position of women in the class structure is a subject worthy of study in its own right. Little is yet known about women's images of class. As in some other spheres of life, the knowledge codified in 'the literature' relates almost wholly to the male half of the population. The female's role has traditionally centred around home and family and her status in the wider society, apart from simply being a woman, has been regarded as dependent upon her husband's. This may be changing and the topic deserves investigation but it was not one of the problems which our enquiry addressed.

As will be seen when the results are presented, the interviews ranged over a number of areas including respondents' career histories, various aspects of their present jobs, political affiliations, religious beliefs, family life and leisure behaviour. Details of the questions phrased will be given as the results are narrated. However, the main problem faced in designing the interviews derived from the fact that we were collecting a large amount of information from approximately five hundred individuals and, therefore, the schedule had to be standardised. This presented little difficulty with questions soliciting straightforward factual information or views on specific issues. The main challenge lay in operationalising the class imagery concept.

The technical difficulties involved in exploring subjective aspects of stratification are considerable, the main problems being to uncover individuals' 'real' views and feelings. It is well known that the likelihood of persons describing themselves as 'middle class' can be varied depending upon the alternative labels offered. One solution involves an investigator avoiding structured questions, proceeding informally, and allowing his subjects to express themselves in their own words. Previous studies examining images of class have nearly all approached the subject in this manner, and data have been analysed into categories constructed after scrutinising respondents' actual statements. This procedure has obvious advantages since images of class can be complex and varied, and investigators wish neither to 'lead' informants nor to force their statements into predetermined and misleading categories. In dealing with a large number of cases, however, as was necessary to tackle the issues at stake in our enquiry, simply recording respondents' answers verbatim and then attempting an analysis would have been impractical.

After two sets of pilot interviews and lengthy discussion, we settled upon a set of questions none of which 'led' respondents, always leaving the initiative in suggesting particular class arrangements in their hands, but which ensured that all aspects of class imagery in which we were interested would be probed and recorded by the interviewers if respondents did not spontaneously volunteer the relevant information. We began by asking each subject whether he believed in the existence of social classes or, if not, other 'significant social differences', thus placing upon interviewees the onus of declaring that there was a class structure that could be further discussed. Virtually every respondent (96 per cent) agreed that classes (or other significant social differences) existed and they were then invited to name the groups to which they belonged, from which point the questioning moved outwards, with many subjects volunteering much of the additional information required without further prompting, to obtain each individual's views about the composition of the remainder of the class structure. At each stage it was the respondents' own answers that were allowed to suggest further issues to be probed and, by proceeding in this manner, we sought to avoid artificially manufacturing images of class.

When respondents agreed that classes or equivalent social differences existed, a total of fourteen further aspects of their views on social class, along which variations had been noted in previous empirical work, were probed. Across these questions we received a few sets of internally contradictory answers, as when individuals who placed themselves in the bottom class later claimed to be in a higher class than their fathers but 85 per cent maintained consistency. Although it is no thorough test of the issue, this constitutes some evidence that the images of class we collected were not randomly conjectured under pressures of the research situation, but corresponded to ideas already present in our subjects' minds.

Even if the answers obtained to our questions on class had been grouped only dichotomously, the fourteen items employed could potentially have led to over 16,000 different images of class occurring. Fortunately the presumption underlying the exercise was vindicated; while we identified more dimensions of variation than are recognised in existing theoretically derived typologies, we found, as have all previous students of class imagery, that our respondents' answers fell into a limited number of clusters enabling distinct types of class imagery to be constructed. For example, when individuals placed themselves in the bottom class, they almost invariably called it the 'working class', claimed that this class was the largest and recognised the existence of only one other class. In our analysis we have labelled this cluster of answers 'proletarian imagery'. One other type of working class imagery and three types of middle class imagery were also identified and details will be given as the argument develops. What must be stressed at this point is that, although grounded upon data obtained from interviews, the varieties of class imagery we discerned are nevertheless ideal types. No two respondents presented totally identical views on the class structure, and the images that we will discuss should be treated as ideal typifications of the several directions in one of which each respondent's views tended to be oriented.

As we will demonstrate, by using these ideal types it is possible to see how certain configurations of objective conditions nurture particular types of subjective response, which in turn enable us to explain the types of political and industrial action towards which groups situated at different levels in the class structure are oriented. Thus the way in which objective features of the system of stratification are either consolidated or changed is revealed. We will illustrate how this type of analysis enables the significance of changes in the circumstances of different groups of both white and blue-collar workers in contemporary society to be grasped.

Strictly our results and conclusions can be shown to apply only at the time and place where the investigation was conducted. So are we justified in addressing more general problems? First, could not the area studied be untypical of the rest of the country? Are we entitled to generalise on the basis of our findings? The answer is that it depends upon the types of generalisations attempted. In certain respects the area selected for enquiry was deliberately chosen because its population was unrepresentative of the wider public. For the purpose of the enquiry it was unnecessary, for example, that the proportion of semi-skilled manual workers in the sample should mirror their representation in the wider society. We cannot, therefore, offer general answers to 'How many?' questions, but our investigation was not intended to contribute towards this type of social book-keeping. Our interest lay not in establishing the proportion of white-collar workers in the area who were trade unionists, or the proportion of manual employees who owned cars and washing machines. The hypotheses we were seeking to test were of the 'if-then' rather than the 'how many?' variety. We were interested in not *how many* but *which* white-collar workers join trade unions, and our concern was not with how many manual workers' earnings exceed a given amount but with the consequences in terms of attitudes and life-styles of different levels of material well-being. In order to support this type of generalisation, it is not necessary that the composition of a sample should be representative of any wider population. What is important is that the sample should offer adequate numbers of subjects in the circumstances required to test the hypotheses being examined and the area selected for our study was chosen with this consideration in mind.

Second, from a survey conducted at one particular point in time, is it possible to drawn any conclusions about the directions and effects of social change? Again, the answer is that it depends upon the type of reasoning involved. From a cross-sectional survey it is certainly not possible to draw a line from some point in the past to the present and carry the graph forward. However, there are other ways of clarifying on-going currents of change. No one can forecast the future with certainty but we know, for example, quite independently of our own enquiry, that real wage and salary levels are edging upwards and that the mean number of years' schooling received by the working population is increasing. If we can establish the consequences of these developments at any one point in time, this provides a base for estimating the societal implications as the developments in question become more widespread and this is the manner in which the evidence from our enquiry will be treated.

In analysing the data from our field work we have computed literally hundreds of tables but, following the standard economical practice, the following text presents only the findings and figures relevant to our main conclusions. All the tables constructed were tested for statistical significance using the chi-square formula, and we have taken account of the statistical significance of our various findings in developing conclusions. However, the results of these significance tests are not given in the tables reproduced below, first because there are no points in the narrative where the entire argument hinges upon whether the difference between two columns of figures happens to be significant at, for example, the 0·01 level, and second because when statistical findings are being published selectively (as is necessary for reasons of cost and readability) we feel that repeatedly claiming statistical significance for the findings being presented tends to impute a spurious validity to the conclusions drawn and we would prefer our arguments to stand without this type of support. Thirdly, for purposes of publication data have been combined in many of the tables presented in the text.

What is social class?

Giddens has noted that 'anyone who has the temerity to write about the theory of social class is immediately plunged into controversy by the very way he approaches his subject—by the materials he chooses to consider and by what he ignores.'[10] Hence the possibility of critics disputing whether the subject-matter of this book, which focuses upon stratification amongst the working population, really merits description as a study of social class. Anyone writing about social class faces a conceptual muddle and this is so despite class being one of the most widely used variables in sociological research. In exploring the hierarchical arrangement of social life, sociologists have a variety of terms at their disposal including class, stratification and inequality. Instead of leading to precision, however, this conceptual richness has generated confusion.

Arguments about the meaning of the term class were fashioned during sociology's formative years. Marx defined classes as collectivities standing in common relationships to the means of production and subsequent disciples have insisted upon retaining the purity of the master's terminology. Thus Wesolowski,[11] along with other communist writers, recognises that differences of income, prestige, education and life-style continue under socialism, yet vehemently insists that these societies are nevertheless classless. Western sociologists, however, have found other uses for the term class. For example, they have distinguished economic classes from occupational classes and social classes, but such fashions have generated little enthusiasm amongst writers with Marxist sympathies who continue to argue that, in 'class societies' at any rate, other systems of inequality are largely shadows cast by more fundamental formations standing in particular relationships to the means of production.

The validity of this Marxian position is, of course, a genuine issue with which sociologists can be properly concerned. Problems arise only when the genuine issue is vulgarised into an argument about the correct use of words. And this easily occurs for, as Ossowski has observed, '... in the course of the nineteenth and twentieth centuries the term (class) itself has acquired a considerable emotional load and a rich field of associations. It is no longer a matter of indifference which denotata receive their share of this emotional charge'.[12] To the rulers of communist societies, therefore, it is no minor semantic issue when they insist that although stratified their societies are nonetheless classless. The legitimacy of their regimes has come to be based upon the claim that theirs are classless societies.

Sociologists, like other men, possess political convictions and, hence, the heat generated by the question 'What is social class?' Simply asserting rival definitions and conceptual schemes, however, is really an idle pastime. There is an alternative and, we believe, preferable way in which sociology can proceed. Conceptions of social class can be presented as *authors'* definitions rather than *the* definitions. The question 'What is social class?' is really incapable of definitive answer. Examiners continue to test sociology students' wits by asking 'What is social class?' In the final analysis, however, this is a non-issue. Definitions are never more than conceptually more-or-less convenient proposals, and sociologists should be able to recognise this even if laymen and political propagandists are not.

It is worth pointing out that the fundamental concern of the classical writers, including Marx, in expounding their definitions of social class was to explore the inter-relationships between the economic, political and other factors involved in systems of stratification. These are the real issues that sociology should be continuing to address and our study directly confronts issues of this type. Arguing about definitions is an unnecessary distraction. There is no sense in which stipulative definitions can be right or wrong. Our definitions are presented below, and given the emotions that surround the subject, some readers will inevitably find them disagreeable. However, we hope it will be recognised that it is only the substantive conclusions rather than our semantics that are really worth disputing.

We are employing *stratification* as a general term to refer to the processes of interplay between the variables involved in systems of inequality. Differences in wealth, income and other factors that individuals order hierarchically are referred to as *inequalities*, the structures of which can be ascertained independently of individuals' subjective assessments. Aggregates of individuals located at particular points in such systems of inequality are called *strata*. *Classes* are defined as the collectivities with which individuals identify themselves in making the hierarchical environments they inhabit meaningful. Thus stratification refers to *processes* from which class *formations* arise and manual workers constitute a stratum but may or may not be a class. We believe that it is useful to distinguish between inequality and class, reserving the latter term for collectivities that are meaningful for their members. The phase *class awareness* will be used, at a minimal level, to indicate the barest recognition on an individual's part that along with others he is positioned a given level in a hierarchically organised society and without such a minimal degree of class awareness, needless to say, no social differences would count as inequalities as defined above. The term *class consciousness* will be reserved for cases where individuals not only acknowledge their location at a given level in the social hierarchy but reciprocate each other's feelings and regard themselves as sharing interests in common that divide them from other classes. Thus classes may be aware in different ways with class consciousness being but one possibility and *class imagery* is a second-order concept that is being used in analysing information about class awareness.

Weinberg and Lyons[13] have noted a hiatus between theoretical controversies about class and the operational definitions used in research which have been extremely varied, though it should be noted that the correlations between the indices commonly used are high, and therefore it is unlikely that sociologists have been so facile as to confuse quite different phenomena. Nevertheless, Weinberg and Lyons call for greater standardisation and also advocate explicitly relating operational definitions of class to theoretical issues. Like ourselves, no doubt in principle all sociologists will agree with this clarion call. However, calling for standardisation begs the question of whose standards. We would be agreeably pleased but also surprised if our concepts were universally adopted. Similarly, asking for definitions to be related to theoretical issues begs the question of which theories. The ways in which we have measured class are explicitly related to issues about stratification in contemporary society that we believe are worth resolving. To expect everyone to agree that the questions we have posed are *the* issues, however, would be naively optimistic.

2. White and Blue Collar

The middle/working class dichotomy

Sociologists have been accused of an obsession with social class.[1] Regardless of the area of social life in which their prime concern lies—delinquency, religion, trade unionism or leisure behaviour—before their investigations are far advanced sociologists can be relied upon to have explored the implications of individuals' social class positions. The importance attached to social class amongst sociologists outstrips levels of class awareness amongst the public at large, hence the obsessive appearance of the sociologists' interest. Sociologists may rarely fail to uncover ramifications of class whatever corners of social life are explored yet the public remains sceptical and while it may test their patience, this indicates a need for sociologists to state the grounds for their interest in the clearest possible terms.

This is nowhere more evident than with the sociological habit of dichotomising the population into working and middle classes and thereby, although multiple criteria are sometimes employed, usually distinguishing manual or blue-collar from non-manual or white-collar workers together with their families. How often do casual references to the working and middle classes provoke rhetorical reminders of dockers who earn more than school-teachers and how frequently are we instantly challenged to place self-employed artisans, small shopkeepers and laboratory assistants?

Even individuals who describe themselves as 'working' or 'middle class' are liable to protest when these labels are applied by sociologists. And the latter have no cause for surprise, for they themselves have devoted volumes to explaining how, in modern societies, there is a prevalent feeling that positions should be achieved rather than ascribed. Hence the affront to many people's values when assigned to a social class by criteria over which they have no control. In the interests of meaningful communication sociologists cannot too frequently stress that their working/middle class dichotomy is not dictating but, to a large extent, is merely following the public's own practice and there is similar value in emphasising that the use of these terms does not imply that the split between a middle and a working class is the sole class division in society, nor that the break between the two is crystal clear. Sociologists are the last group to need reminding that some individuals are difficult to place. Once these disclaimers have been expressed it is easier to argue that, nevertheless, the working and middle class concepts are not arbitrarily conjectured labels but correspond to a genuine break in the social hierarchy. Whatever the trends, there are three major blocks of evidence, corroborated by the results of our own enquiry, which indicate that this schism is still very much alive.

The first is that most manual workers describe themselves as 'working class' while the majority of white-collar employees assign themselves to a 'middle class' and members of the public have not learnt these phrases from sociology. This subject may have publicised them, but the terms entered common usage in the nineteenth century before sociology even properly existed.

In our investigation, as in all comparable predecessors in both Britain and America,[2] in response to a direct question nearly every subject agreed that society was divided into social classes. Furthermore, in reply to an open-ended question few respondents proved unable or unwilling to name the classes to which they belonged and in over four out of five cases the terms 'middle' or 'working class' featured in these self-descriptions. Needless to say, matters were not quite so simple as this implies. Many respondents prefixed these class labels to locate themselves, for example, in a lower middle or upper middle class. As will be argued in later chapters, both the terms 'middle' and 'working class' can mean different things to different people. To complicate matters still further, the widespread use of these terms does not indicate public consensus on the shape and composition of the class structure, for the self-assigned memberships of our working and middle classes tended to give asymmetrical meanings to these phrases. As will become evident as the data are presented, the working class with which individuals identify is most frequently considered the largest stratum located at the base of a pyramid-shaped class structure, but the middle class to which individuals who use the phrase assign themselves is usually not considered a relatively narrow stratum situated in the upper half of a pyramid. It is more frequently defined as the largest class covering the middle ground in a diamond-like hierarchy.

Needless to say, because individuals are prepared to label themselves as middle or working class when invited by sociologists, it does not necessarily follow that they ordinarily think in these terms during their everyday lives. Sociologists are well aware of this, call the problem one of *salience*, and have devoted some energy to its investigation. One view contends that salience is greater amongst the working than the middle class or, in other words, that the former is the more strongly class aware,[3] while another theory suggests that the salience of social class has been declining over the last generation[4] and that

Table 2:1
Corollaries of occupational status

	Registrar General's social class					
	1 n = 39	2 n = 121	3NM n = 83	3M n = 145	4 n = 63	5 n = 23
Self-assigned class						
% middle	74	71	48	37	21	29
% working	11	23	42	56	66	62
Party supported at previous general election						
% Conservative	67	78	65	32	29	12
% Labour	24	22	34	65	71	88
Occupational association membership						
% trade union members	26	30	57	72	83	57

Note: 1) Social class 3NM = 3 Non-manual
Social class 3M = 3 Manual
2) 'Other' and 'Non' categories have been omitted.

we may be moving towards a state that Dennis Wrong has termed 'inequality without stratification',[5] but the evidence on both these points is still ambiguous.

These embellishments to the picture are interesting, but the fact remains that most members of the public and of our sample chose to locate themselves in either a middle or a working class and, as one moves down the occupational hierarchy, the point at which the majority begin to prefer the 'working-class' label roughly coincides with the cross-over between the white-collar and manual strata (see Table 2:1).

Occupations are not the only factors influencing the social classes with which individuals identify. In his survey on sex and marriage,

Geoffrey Gorer found that 40 per cent of the women interviewed but only 26 per cent of the men described themselves as middle class.[6] Women are the more likely to identify themselves 'up' the social scale and this says something about sex differences in contemporary society, but it does not deny the relationship between occupations and self-assigned class that is found amongst each sex.

The second block of evidence concerns the public's party political loyalties. In Britain the majority of non-manual workers and their families vote Conservative whereas, with the sharpest shift in loyalties again roughly coinciding with the transition between the white and blue-collar strata, amongst manual workers support for the Labour Party is dominant. Needless to say, there are many cases of 'deviance'. The association between occupational status and both self-assigned class and party political preference is a powerful tendency but a far from universal rule. There are professional people who describe themselves as 'working class' and vote Labour just as there are 'middle class' manual workers who support the Conservative Party and such deviants have attracted almost as much comment as the general tendency.

Blue-collar deviance from the class norm is rather more common than deviance amongst the non-manual strata, a fact of some importance if only because it is this that makes British party politics a genuine contest. Since manual workers and their families comprise the majority of the population, if everyone voted according to their class norm the Labour Party would be the inevitable victor in every general election. In practice, however, throughout the country blue-collar defectors outweigh white-collar deviants and give the Conservative Party approximately a half of its total electoral support, thus creating a 'balanced' political arena. The exceptions to the rule, therefore, cannot be dismissed as insignificant, but the same applies with equal force to the existence of class norms in voting behaviour.

The third block of evidence that the middle/working class split is a real cleavage in the social structure concerns trade union membership. Over 50 per cent of all manual employees in Britain are trade unionists whereas membership is considerably less dense amongst white-collar workers. The public comment that the recent 'growth of white-collar trade unionism' has attracted rightly emphasises, once again, that there are numerous deviant cases, but the discrepancy between overall levels of unionisation amongst the blue and white-collar strata remains considerable.[7]

The incidence of exceptional cases does not lessen the value of the middle/working class dichotomy, but in certain ways actually increases its utility, for a significant feature of the deviant instances is their tendency to cluster. For example, blue-collar workers who deviate by describing themselves as 'middle class' tend to be the same individuals who deviate from their class norm as regards politics and trade union membership.[8] Self-assigned class, party political loyalties and trade union membership, therefore, are not only all similarly associated with occupational status but are also related to each other, thus producing *syndromes* characteristic of the working and middle classes respectively. Manual workers tend to describe themselves as working class and when they do so they are exceptionally likely to vote for the Labour Party and belong to a trade union. Conversely white-collar workers tend to align themselves with a middle class, in which case the likelihood of support for the Conservative Party and their remaining outside the trade union movement become especially strong and it is this overall pattern into which the evidence falls that makes it meaningful to talk about middle and working class *values*. The white/blue collar split corresponds not only to differences in terms and conditions of employment, but additionally taps a cleavage of an ideological character which relates to industrial strategies and political affiliations. Endorsement of working class values is not evenly spread throughout the manual strata and support for middle class values is similarly uneven amongst white-collar workers. There are individual manual workers whose values approximate more closely to those of the middle rather than the working class and vice versa. But this in no sense negates the evidence indicating that the manual strata harbour a distinctive set of working class values while the white-collar strata prove hospitable to middle class values and this is the justification for dichotomising the population into middle and working classes.

In the USA the white/blue collar split, in terms of political affiliations for example, is less sharp than in Western Europe,[9] but to some degree this cleavage occurs in the class structures of all industrial societies. Even in the Soviet Union it is conventional to note the difference between 'workers' and 'employees' and if the middle/working class divide appears especially prominent in Britain this is not so much because Britain's class structure is exceptionally rigid, but rather because other possible points of division are less active. With only 3 per cent of the labour force in agriculture, Britain is too extensively urbanised for a town/country division to be politically important, outside Ulster religious differences hardly intrude into political and economic life, while up to the present ethnicity has remained an issue only of 'community relations'. Given the paucity of the competition, observers will be left understandably impressed by the

prominence of class divisions in Britain, but there is no industrial
society in which the terms working and middle class or equivalents
are not in currency nor, outside the communist world, where trade
union membership is as dense amongst white as blue-collar
workers,[10] nor where party political preferences show no variation
between these sections of the population.

One nation?

When laymen can be persuaded to admit that the middle/working
class division is not merely a figment of sociologists' imaginations,
the admission is often tinged with qualifications. Politicians hoping
to cultivate a national appeal transcending class boundaries are particularly liable to argue that the division is merely a legacy from the
past and that it has ceased to correspond to any real conflict of interest. The idea that affluence, the welfare state and related developments are transforming Britain into 'one nation' lends credibility to
the view that there is little reason any longer why manual and white-
collar workers should identify with different classes and that before
long the terms 'middle' and 'working class' will appear only in history
books.

The likely directions of contemporary change will be discussed in
a subsequent chapter, but what needs demonstrating immediately
is the persistence of sharp differences of circumstance and interest
between white and blue-collar workers. Despite what some commentators might believe, the plain fact is that manual workers remain
excluded from a whole range of privileges that the middle classes
have long taken for granted.

a) *Pay*: Contrary to widespread belief, the economic status of
white-collar workers is still relatively privileged. During 1975 the press
carried stories of £300 per week welders driving 'E' type Jaguars to
the picket lines in support of their claim for parity with even better-
paid tradesmen and during no period during the last twenty years
have such tales been in short supply. Car-workers, dockers and
miners have successively received their share of the headlines. Powerful trade unions with militant leaders and avaricious shop stewards
have been portrayed as overturning not only traditional differentials
but also the national interest. In successive appeals for pay restraint
the blue-collar trade unionist has consistently figured as the villain.
It is probably not surprising, therefore, that repeated surveys should
have found white-collar employees expressing concern at being not
only overtaken but left behind.[11] Exactly how, why and with what

effects this impression has been created will be discussed more fully later. For the meantime, however, it is sufficient to record that the facts are less dramatic than the talk.

There are three major points to be set against the widespread view of the white-collar worker being overtaken. The first is simply that an overlap between the earnings of blue and white-collar workers is not a new phenomenon but has existed since the nineteenth century. The counting house clerk was never more highly paid than the skilled tradesman.[12] He enjoyed other advantages such as the status associated with education and literacy, job security and holidays with pay but his earnings were often inferior. Likewise the nineteenth-century elementary school-teacher rarely earned more than a skilled artisan.[13] When present-day teachers bemoan their declining status they rather ingenuously use the nineteenth-century secondary school-master as a basis for comparison. An overlap between blue and white-collar earnings is no recent development and any extension of this overlap has been no more than marginal. The most impressive feature of trends in pay differentials over time has been their stability and on average, although an overlap persists, white-collar workers continue to earn more.[14] This is shown to be the case in the data published regularly by the Department of Employment. In November 1974 the Department's Gazette reported average earnings for male manual workers running at £43·60 per week, while for white-collar workers the comparable figure was £54·40. Furthermore, during the twelve months up to April 1974, white collar earnings increased on average by 15 per cent as against 14·2 per cent for manual workers. These figures have not been deceptively handpicked. The fact is that the view of the white-collar worker being overtaken is, in most cases, a myth whose sustenance is no doubt aided by it being the percentage figure by which blue-collar earnings have risen that invariably attracts more publicity than their continuing lag behind white-collar pay levels.

The second point to be borne in mind concerns the differing shapes of blue and white-collar workers' income careers. This is illustrated in Table 2:2 which shows how white-collar earnings are positively related to age and how individuals can normally hope to enjoy progressive careers, increasing their earning power and standards of living throughout their working lives. The manual worker, in contrast, has often reached his career ceiling by the time he is in his early twenties and earning the full adult rate for his job and can only expect the real value of his earnings to rise if his occupational group or the entire community experiences a growth in prosperity. Table 2:2 shows that at the outset of their careers there may be little difference between the spread of incomes amongst blue and white-collar employees, but by the time a cohort is over the age of thirty, non-manual workers' progressive careers are pushing their earnings ahead. One effect of this white-collar income career pattern is to provide a cushion against the family poverty cycle.

With marriage, the arrival of children and wives relinquishing paid employment, real standards of life are threatened, but the white-collar workers' growing earning power can offset these changes in family circumstances. For the blue-collar worker, however, Margaret Wynn has demonstrated that the cycle of poverty that was noted in the classical surveys of Charles Booth and Seebohm Rowntree at the beginning of the twentieth century still applies.[15] The value of state welfare benefits far from covers the cost of a family, so during the child-rearing phase of the life-cycle the living standards of blue-

Table 2:2

Occupation and income careers

	Date of birth					
	White-collar			Blue-collar		
Annual income	After 1941 n = 45	1927–41 n = 67	Before 1927 n = 101	After 1941 n = 42	1927–41 n = 85	Before 1927 n = 89
% less than £1500	53	2	9	43	19	42
% £1501–£2000	27	25	21	40	33	40
% £2001–£2500	13	34	24	12	34	9
% £2501 and over	7	39	47	5	14	9

collar households are continuously threatened. There must be some truth in Wynn's suggestion that these facts of working class life can only fuel inflationary wage demands.

During this stage in the life-cycle manual workers are under pressure to maximise earnings and there is evidence that they do so by moving to jobs where good money can be earned even if the work is not intrinsically rewarding, tolerating shift-work and volunteering for whatever overtime is available.[16] Data from our investigation presented in Table 2:3 show that income levels amongst manual workers depend upon the number of hours that they work. The well-paid blue-collar employee often owes his affluence to an actual working week in excess of fifty hours. The earnings of white-collar workers, in contrast, display no consistent association with the length of the working week. The non-manual employee's earning power is much more dependent upon the status of his occupation

Table 2:3
Occupations, hours of work and pay

Annual income	White-collar					Blue-collar				
	51+ n=39	46–50 n=21	42–45 n=34	38–41 n=59	less than 38 n=59	51+ n=39	46–50 n=41	42–45 n=39	38–41 n=91	less than 38 n=10
	%	%	%	%	%	%	%	%	%	%
less than £1500	13	10	15	22	15	18	17	51	42	10
£1501–£2000	18	29	18	25	27	36	56	23	34	50
£2001–£2500	18	24	18	27	31	18	15	26	18	40
£2501 and over	51	38	50	25	27	28	12	—	7	—

Hours normally worked

and the stage he has reached in his career. Not all white-collar workers enjoy a thirty-five-hour week. Amongst self-employed businessmen and independent professionals in particular, long hours are not uncommon. But it is quite possible in a non-manual occupation to find relatively short hours of work combined with high earnings. In contrast, the blue-collar employee's affluence is not delivered by a progressive career: he is visibly obliged to earn it. Following the child-rearing phase of the life-cycle, manual earnings taper off. Individuals are no longer under the same pressure to take whatever overtime is available and may move to lighter and lower paid jobs as their physical powers decline. In contrast, it is during this phase of the white-collar employee's career that his earnings are likely to peak. Whilst blue and white-collar earnings may overlap considerably amongst individuals aged under thirty, in the forty-five plus age group there is hardly any overlap at all. White-collar middle age promises comforts that are unavailable to the blue-collar labour force.

One could summarise this evidence by stating that white-collar workers have careers whereas blue-collar employees simply do jobs. In its conventional meaning the career remains a white-collar privilege, though there is a modest sense in which one can talk of blue-collar careers. During their working lives manual workers may enjoy some experience of career progression. For the apprentice there is the rise to skilled status, while for all there is at least the off-chance of progression to chargehand, foreman or even into self-employment. In addition the manual employee can aim at and sometimes sense achievement by moving to a good firm, a secure job, or one where the work is not particularly onerous. Although they rarely use this terminology blue-collar employees often attach considerable importance to such 'career achievements' and, as Michael Mann has shown, may be willing to uproot their families and move home to avoid forfeiting their career gains.[17] The difference compared with white-collar careers, however, is that amongst blue-collar workers the 'careers' mentioned above are not available to all, the length of the ladders involved is short and the gains are never fully secure. During recent years white-collar redundancy has attracted comment proportionate only to its previous rarity. It is still blue-collar workers, particularly the unskilled, who face the greatest risk of redundancy, unemployment, lay-offs and short-time. Rather than a progressive career, it is these prospects that loom large during the manual employee's working life.

An implication of their progressive careers is that during their working lives nearly all white-collar workers can expect to move into positions where they exercise some authority. In any medium or large-sized organisation, a novice remains the junior for only a few months. Hierarchy is a feature of the white-collar work environment, and during their working lives virtually all employees can expect to exercise authority in addition to being subject to it. Given his typically flat career, however, authority is one of the few resources that the manual worker remains perpetually more likely to receive than dispense.

The third point that qualifies the portrait of the overtaken white-collar worker concerns the implications of the division of labour by sex in employment. Some commentators have correctly drawn attention to the growth of 'proletarian' white-collar occupations in offices and laboratories where incumbents face promotion blockages and the sight of better-qualified recruits not only being promoted but actually entering employment at more senior levels. The occupation of the clerk has been subject to this kind of downgrading since the nineteenth century. But a concomitant trend has been the transformation of routine clerical work from a male into an almost exclusively female occupation.[18] Women, until the present at any rate, have not been expected to demand progressive careers. Their aspirations have been regarded as centred upon home and family and so by recruiting a substantial proportion of female workers, employers have remained able to guarantee career opportunities to male 'staff' recruits. The majority of bank clerks never rise to management, but by arranging an intake substantially composed of females, the leading banks have been able to offer their male intake a one-in-two chance of rising to managerial positions. There are male technicians bristling with frustration at encountering the graduate barrier,[19] and male clerks in industry also complain about their limited career prospects,[20] but the typist, secretary, receptionist and roneo operator is almost invariably a she rather than a he and this pattern of sex discrimination enhances the career prospects of male entrants into white-collar work. Whatever might be widely believed, when all these features of the situation are taken into account, white-collar workers remain relatively privileged not only in the sense that their jobs are the more prestigious, but also in straightforward economic terms.

   b) *Fringe benefits*: In discussing the remuneration of executives, management consultants today are less likely to talk simply about salary levels than overall 'compensation packages'. It is now widely recognised that 'pay' is just one element in the executive's total returns from employment. Other elements can include pension rights, health insurance, use of company vehicles, meals and entertainment, and it is not unusual for the total value of these 'fringe benefits' to account for more than a third of the overall compensation package. When called upon to do so, employers may justify the company car, private medical insurance and trips to night clubs as tools of the trade; essential perquisites enabling the employee to function effectively at his job. Executives themselves, however, acknowledge these benefits as the perks that they are and their popularity is undoubtedly related to a desire shared by both employers and employees to avoid the 'penal' levels of taxation to which earned income is normally liable. Because they are not officially recorded as income for tax purposes, it is difficult to judge the exact value and prevalence of these fringe benefits. And it is equally difficult to see how their provision could be rationally justified to those excluded from the largess. Even if a manager needs to use a motor vehicle in the course of his employment, why should he, rather than any other employee, enjoy the use of the car in question during his leisure?

There may be a widely held view that traditional status distinctions between staff and works are being eroded, and it is true that holidays with pay are no longer exclusively middle class privileges, that the welfare state has made an income during periods of sickness and unemployment into universal rights rather than prerogatives of the few and that along with denim fashions the snob value of wearing street-clothes to work has largely disappeared. It is also becoming increasingly common for manual workers to be raised to salaried status in the sense of being paid monthly and by cheque. During this upgrading, however, the fringe benefits made available to the traditionally salaried staff have not remained static. Wedderburn's research has shown that there are still many fringe benefits that are regarded as normal in the office but which are either unavailable to manual workers or are offered only on a much less generous scale.[21] Wedderburn collected information from a sample of manufacturing firms in 1968 and many of the contrasts revealed between the fringe entitlements of 'operatives' and employees at the lowest level of 'clerical' employment were dramatic. Over fifteen paid holidays per year were enjoyed by clerical workers in 74 per cent of the firms but by operatives in only 38 per cent; 76 per cent allowed clerks to choose their own holiday times but only 35 per cent in the case of operatives. The comparable percentages allowing time off with pay for personal reasons were 83 and 29, while pay deductions for lateness applied to operatives in 90 per cent of the firms but to clerical staff in only 8 per cent.

The picture amongst the sample covered in our own enquiry was similar. In Table 2:4 blue-collar respondents are divided into more and less affluent groups according to whether or not they were earning over £2000 per year at the time of the enquiry, and the point that this illustrates is that even when their income levels reach the 'middle class' bracket, manual workers become no more liable to receive white-collar fringe benefits. The figures focus upon benefits that, in principle, have a measurable economic value, but there are additional distinctions between blue and white-collar conditions of employment that are not so easily quantified. There are few factories in which managers do not enjoy the use of better-appointed canteens and toilets than the blue-collar workforce—and where the office en-

Table 2:4

Occupations, incomes and fringe benefits

| | Annual income | | |
| | Blue-collar workers | | White-collar workers |
Benefits	up to £2000 p.a. n = 152	over £2000 p.a. n = 64	n = 243
% receiving full pay during 2 weeks sickness	56	41	75
% enjoying 'travel facilities' as a fringe benefit	40	32	55
% whose holiday entitlement (excluding bank holidays) exceeds 21 days	20	25	55

vironment is not more congenial than conditions on the shop-floor which, as many observers have remarked, often remain conducive to a spirit of solidarity that underwrites support for working class institutions such as trade unions and the Labour Party. To a large extent status differences in working conditions are technically unavoidable, but this in no way alters the fact that white-collar workers are 'cosseted' to an extent that is beyond the bounds of possibility for most blue-collar employees. From time to time the problem of 'scroungers' on the welfare state provokes predictably outraged press comment. How can the economy afford such indolence? Whatever the scale of this so-called problem its economic effects are minimal compared with the syphoning-off that occurs in the form of middle class fringe benefits.

These benefits may be 'fringe' in terms of their manner of provision, but they are anything but fringe according to the scale of their consequences. It is by no means unusual for managers and professional people to retire on half-pay, an amount that will often exceed average blue-collar earnings, in addition to the benefits they are entitled to under the state's national insurance scheme. This contrasts starkly with the prospects that face many manual workers upon retirement; a standard of life around the minimum 'poverty' line considered tolerable by the Department of Social Security. It is not a pleasant prospect, but it is one that millions have to look forward to.

c) *Housing and life-styles*: The economic inequalities outlined above carry inevitable implications for individuals' lives outside the workplace and this is one reason why social class differences extend into virtually every corner of life. The ways in which social class

Table 2 : 5

Occupations and housing

Housing class	Occupational category	
	White-collar n = 243	*Blue-collar* n = 231
	%	%
Owner-occupier	72	33
Council tenant	8	52
Other	20	15

affects such spheres of life as educational opportunity and uses of leisure are too manifold to be comprehensively analysed at this point, but one basic class-related inequality that requires emphasis concerns access to housing. From time to time there is talk of Britain becoming a property-owning democracy and an image is conjured of a society in which home-ownership is entering the grasp of the entire population. There is also talk, though probably more in America than Britain, of a merging of previously distinct social classes in the suburban owner-occupied estates that have been described as new 'melting pots'. Engaging though it may be, however, this kind of talk is far removed from the persistent realities of life that confront most blue-collar families.

Our survey was conducted in a suburban area which, from census data, might have appeared to be acting as a melting pot. The population was socially mixed with residents drawn from all levels in the occupational hierarchy, but closer inspection revealed considerable segregation along social class lines within the area. As Table 2 : 5 shows, most of the white-collar workers in our sample were owner-occupiers and instances where this was not the case usually involved young, unmarried men. The blue-collar respondents, in contrast, were mainly in rented accommodation and in most such cases the landlord was the local council. Traditional working class city-centre areas may be in the process of demolition, but the construction of replacement blue-collar ghettoes in the suburbs is well under way. There were some blue-collar owner-occupiers in our sample, but they were the exceptions to the rule.

Few white-collar workers fail to appreciate that home-ownership is a sound investment. Buying one's own home makes good economic sense. However, unless there is a radical change in the political economy of home-ownership, it is doubtful whether this status can become a viable proposition for most manual workers in Britain during the near future. Unlike many of the middle class families studied by Colin Bell,[22] working class families are rarely able to transmit property down the generations to assist recently married couples to purchase their own homes. Defenders of 'middle class values' might ask why working class couples cannot learn to save, but this ignores the fact that the sum required as deposit upon a house constitutes wealth surpassing the aspirations that most working class households will ever have entertained. Working class couples tend to marry and embark upon parenthood at younger ages than is common in middle class circles and in addition to houses there are other things to be saved for, including cars and holidays. Furthermore, the building societies display a partiality towards young men with qualifications who are embarking upon progressive careers, whose incomes are secure and are expected to grow. There are too many institutional and cultural barriers to make home-ownership for the majority of manual workers imminent. So the blue-collar employee is not only a second-class citizen at work and in terms of the distribution of economic privilege, but is also relegated to a second-class or even lower division in terms of chances in the housing market with inevitable implications for the quality of family and community life that he is able to enjoy.

Social class and commonsense

Defining one's terms carefully is usually sound advice. So far, however, we have skirted the question of exactly what constitutes a white or blue-collar worker. We have deferred the problem partly because these concepts are notoriously difficult to define, but also to give a practical illustration that it is possible to use these terms in a comprehensible discussion without offering formal definitions.

It is self-evident that the expressions blue and white-collar, manual and non-manual, are not meant to be taken literally. Where would one place a dental surgeon if operating a literal interpretation of the manual/non-manual schism? Nearly all occupations demand a combination of physical and mental effort, the way in which people dress to work does not really suggest a clean break between the middle and working classes and neither does any other single aspect of workers' terms and conditions of employment. Scholarly articles have been written noting that, despite their common usage, no one has yet provided definitions of the manual and non-manual concepts sufficiently precise to be operationalised in empirical research.[23]

Yet paradoxically, despite well-known problem cases that are difficult to classify, few members of the public experience great difficulty if asked to place most occupations and their incumbents into either a manual or a non-manual category. This is so because being conversant with the everyday culture of their own society, individuals simply 'know' where particular occupations are located and feel competent classifiers although unable to precisely articulate the reasons for their decisions. This is why the above discussion will have been understandable despite the absence of formal definitions of key terms that are literally imprecise. It is also the reason why a purely commonsensical grading of occupations, such as the Registrar General's, which we are using to analyse our survey results, can 'work' in the sense of possessing a proven predictive power and has been widely used in social research for over half a century despite lacking any coherent theoretical justification.

No single variable distinguishes what are commonly thought of as the blue and white-collar sectors and expecting precise definitions of these terms misunderstands the reality of the situations to which they refer. Rather than any single factor, the terms blue and white-collar refer to *configurations* of inter-related circumstances including those described above. To be a manual worker is to be employed in a particular type of occupation, but its everyday meaning also implies enjoying a certain level and type of remuneration and career prospects and living in a certain type of house located in a particular kind of district. One can refer to those who share these circumstances as a working class because they tend to share a common class identity and subscribe to common working class values which encompass support for trade unions and the Labour Party. Ordinary members of society are intuitively aware of these configurations and, therefore, are not puzzled when concepts such as blue and white-collar are introduced in everyday conversation and sociologists who divide the population into middle and working classes are not imposing their own, alien professional concepts upon a quite different reality, but are simply making explicit what is ordinarily more vaguely known and taken for granted.

Irrespective of arguments concerning historical trends, any inspection of the evidence demonstrates that the manual worker still occupies an underdog status and however loud their complaints about being overtaken, there are no signs of the middle class clamouring to become car-workers, dockers and miners. To regard oneself as middle class necessarily implies an awareness of the existence of subordinate strata, while identification with the working class implies that the main division in society of which individuals are conscious separates those like themselves from more privileged classes and the fact that this type of awareness remains prevalent amongst manual workers is not difficult to explain once the evidence is squarely faced. Across all major areas of social experience including income from employment, virtually every type of fringe benefit and access to housing, the manual worker remains the underdog and it would be surprising if the individuals affected remained oblivious to this fact. The evidence of a working class culture nurturing distinct working class values is but a reflection and response to crude material disadvantages. Whatever the trends, there are no signs that the eradication of these disadvantages is imminent and, therefore, there are no valid grounds for arguing that the middle/working class dichotomy is outdated.

3. The Embourgeoisement Thesis and its Critics

Sociologists may be agreed that the working/middle class division indicates a real cleavage in the social structure but beyond this point they divide into a panorama of debate. How deep is the cleavage? What are the historical trends? Are there additional schisms within the middle and working classes? These are controversial issues. As regards the working class, it is generally acknowledged that blue-collar workers are not homogeneously involved in a working class culture. Hence questions arise concerning the main dimensions of variation and, related to this, the directions of change over time.

The embourgeoisement thesis

These questions have produced contending answers including one known as the embourgeoisement thesis. The term embourgeoisement refers to a process whereby manual workers are absorbed and assimilated into the middle classes and one school of thought claims to have identified this as a contemporary trend. There can be no denying the fact that some blue-collar workers display bourgeois characteristics. Surveys repeatedly reveal manual workers who assign themselves to a middle class, remain outside the trade unions and vote Conservative. In the debate surrounding the embourgeoisement thesis, however, the existence of bourgeois manual workers is not at issue. Exponents of the thesis do not simply note the existence of these cases. The crucial claim is that the development of bourgeois attitudes amongst manual workers is related to their enjoyment of material circumstances that were once prerogatives of the white-collar strata. It is alleged that the absorption of manual workers into the middle class in terms of attitudes, social relationships and life-styles is a result of their growing ability to share middle class privileges that were once available only to white-collar workers. Hence the predicted scenario of rising income levels, the demise of authoritarian management in the face of powerful trade unions, the growth of educational opportunities and the spread of home-ownership operating as catalysts fostering bourgeois attitudes and life-styles.

One part of the embourgeoisement argument is uncontroversial; namely, that some manual workers and particularly their children must be drawn into the white-collar strata as a result of changes in the occupational structure. Blue-collar employees are gradually comprising a smaller proportion of the working population. In 1900 80 per cent of the population in Britain consisted of manual workers and their families but this figure has now declined to around 60 per cent, while in the USA blue-collar workers are already a minority of the labour force. Developments inherent in the growth of an industrial economy progressively increase the relative size of the white-collar sector. As society becomes increasingly prosperous economic activity switches from primary, extractive industries such as mining and agriculture, to the secondary, manufacturing sector and subsequently to services including health and education in which the labour force is predominantly white-collar. In addition, technological progress creates new scientific and technical occupations while reducing the demand for crude muscle power and the growth in size of employing organisations results in new armies of administrators, executives and clerks. All other things being equal, therefore, the centre of gravity in the political system seems certain to shift rightwards, while trade unions seem destined to find themselves either having to recruit white-collar workers in greater numbers than in the past or ceasing to represent the bulk of the working population and becoming just a minority pressure group.

Needless to say, there are plenty of grounds for suspecting that all other things will not remain equal. Indeed, one view, that will be considered in a later chapter, argues that some sections of the growing white-collar strata are being proletarianised. However, the fact that the manual strata are in decline as a proportion of the labour force is not in dispute, but the central argument contained within the embourgeoisement thesis, that changes amongst the manual workers that remain will accentuate the decline of the working class, is more controversial.

This latter claim has been receiving periodic support since the nineteen-fifties from a succession of investigators who have studied apparently advanced sections of the working class, including employees in the growth industries of the fifties like steel and electrical goods, and the highly paid car-makers of the sixties.[1] More general surveys of the social landscape, some of cross-national character, have also endorsed the embourgeoisement thesis. Rather than a pyramid with a large working class located beneath a smaller middle class, the forecast shape of the class structure is portrayed as a diamond with sections of both the manual and white-collar strata merged into a new and numerically dominant middle class. The Westleys have argued that such developments are already pronounced in America, that similar trends can be discerned in Europe, and they construct an archetype of the emerging worker who, we are assured, will become increasingly common throughout advanced industrial societies.[2] We are offered a vision of the future in which the numerically dominant group in the class structure will be a middle stratum of mostly semi-skilled but highly paid manual and office workers who live in suburbia, benefit from the periodic retraining necessary in an advanced economy and share a common mass consumption life-style within which there are variations in quantity depending upon income but not differences in quality. Writers who claim to have identified such a trend do not predict the demise of all social conflict and dissent. It is not envisaged that the new, broad middle stratum will be exactly like the old middle class. New types of problems are forecast as, for example, educational opportunities and the right to participate in decision-making at work that were previously claimed only by a small middle class become mass demands. The forecast is not the advent of an age of social harmony, but of traditional working class issues being replaced by different problems.[3]

Perhaps more than anywhere else the embourgeoisement thesis has captured the imaginations of political commentators. The Labour Party's series of electoral defeats during the nineteen-fifties when the Conservatives won three consecutive general elections created a situation to which the embourgeoisement thesis apparently offered an explanation. A working class that had 'never had it so good' seemed to herald the permanent decline of distinctly working class politics. Political analysts claimed that with the erosion of the traditional working class, a Labour Party that retained a working class image was destined to find its electoral base suffering similar erosion. Hence even sympathetic observers advised the Labour Party of a need either to update its policies so as to transform its image and broaden its electoral appeal, or face the future as a permanent minority force.[4]

A new working class?

Although it has commanded considerable attention, it would be misleading to imply that the embourgeoisement thesis has ever won general favour amongst sociologists. Restatements of the thesis have been repeatedly matched by debunking comment. In both America and Britain, suburban housing developments have provoked excited arguments about classless melting pots, but rival studies of manual workers in these locations have consistently remarked upon their capacity to conserve working class attitudes and to remain apart from middle class social networks.[5] Sceptics have observed that a washing machine may be primarily a washing machine rather than a status symbol and that it is entirely possible for manual workers to acquire what were formerly middle class incomes and houses without adopting middle class values and without gaining or even aspiring to acceptance as equals by longer-standing members of the middle class. However 'advanced' they may become in other respects, critics of the embourgeoisement thesis have pointed out that manual workers' career patterns and jobs remain distinctly working class.

But whatever their reluctance to admit embourgeoisement, many sociologists have felt it necessary to recognise that during recent decades the working class has been changing. In addition to economic betterment, traditional working class neighbourhoods have disappeared in programmes of urban redevelopment, whilst older regions together with their traditional industries including coal and cotton, once principal mainstays of the labour movement, have been in decline. If not embourgeoisement, might not such changes be creating a new working class?

This train of thought has drawn encouragement from *The Affluent Worker* study,[6] an enquiry undertaken specifically to test the embourgeoisement thesis. The study was conducted in Luton, a 'prototypical' town with modern houses and industries employing affluent workers, and amongst a sample of 229 manual workers at three firms whose industrial experience had commenced only during the prosperous post-war years. In other words, a whole range of prevailing circumstances were expected to favour embourgeoisement. Yet in contrast to the situation amongst a sample of 54 white-collar employees who were studied for comparative purposes, density of trade union membership remained high, support for the Labour Party was more solid than throughout the nationwide manual strata, and there was little evidence of assimilation into middle class social networks. In the face of this evidence the investigators cast the embourgeoisement thesis aside, but not without noting certain differences between their respondents' attitudes towards working class institutions and images of society and those taken to be prevalent amongst more traditional sections of the working class.

In an article written in conjunction with *The Affluent Worker*, David Lockwood distinguishes two traditional working class images of society; one proletarian, the other deferential.[7] Proletarian imagery involves a consciousness of 'us' and 'them', the 'us' being the underdogs. It is the type of 'class ideology' that Elizabeth Bott terms a 'power-model' in which social classes are perceived as differing in power and other privileges, but not in the prestige that would legitimise these inequalities.[8] The accompanying sentiments are collectivist and solidaristic. There is little desire for individual social mobility, but great emphasis upon obtaining a better deal for the entire class to which the individual feels he belongs. There is a strong awareness of the working class sharing collective interests that conflict with those of more privileged strata, and of a consequent need to stand solidly together to defend or further the common cause. Popitz and his collaborators in a study of Ruhr steelworkers have shown that there can be modulations involving varying degrees of both fatalistic acceptance and revolutionary ardour but, as in many other studies of manual workers, amongst the steel-men the 'us–them' image proved a recurrent theme.[9]

Lockwood claims that this type of imagery is likely to be found when large numbers of manual workers and their families are bound together in close-knit occupational and neighbourhood communities sharing similar work experiences and life-styles and set apart from other strata, as has traditionally been the case amongst dockworkers, coalminers and deep-sea fishermen.[10] It is alleged that this type of milieu favours a spirit of comradeship and a consciousness of 'us' set against 'them', thereby awakening feelings of loyalty towards working class organisations such as trade unions and the Labour Party. Cannon offers an illustration of these processes in his study of compositors.[11] He describes how their work situation gives rise to powerful social ties and sentiments, consolidated by frequent 'pass-rounds' and collective outings. The outcome is termed an 'occupational community' which, despite high earnings and the attendant motor cars, telephones and suchlike, conserves feelings of loyalty towards working class institutions. Richard Hoggart is but one amongst many commentators who have lucidly if somewhat romantically described the kind of day-to-day neighbourhood living that can help to consolidate this traditional working class frame of mind.[12] There is an awareness of facing common problems and a need to stick together and the resultant solidarity of the immediate community is seen as provoking the sentiments that are bound into a more generalised proletarian image of society.

Lockwood's second type of traditional working class imagery belongs to the deferential worker who may acknowledge the existence of 'us' and 'them' but differs from the proletarian principally in treating the existing relationships between these classes as legitimate. The deferential worker knows his place and grants betters their due respect; he does not question their claims to privilege and considers it proper that they should lead lesser mortals like himself. Lockwood argues that this type of imagery is prevalent amongst agricultural workers and employees in small-scale industry. Systematically assembled supporting evidence was unavailable and this ideal-type, therefore, derives more from the idea than evidence of the reality of the village labourer accepting his station as part of the natural order. Nevertheless, as Lockwood illustrates, it is possible to construct a persuasive argument alleging that when people live and work immersed not amongst others like themselves but in regular face-to-face contact and relationships of dependence upon superiors, deferential attitudes and similar broader images of society will result.

Lockwood and his co-authors of *The Affluent Worker* argue that, although not bourgeois, in terms of both work and neighbourhood situations and also in terms of their images of society, their Luton informants differed from traditional sections of the working class. The nature of work in large-scale, highly mechanised industry, typified by the assembly line, was considered unconducive to involvement either in the job itself or in solidaristic, 'matey' work-group relationships. In contrast, this type of work appeared liable to attract those who already possessed and, amongst others, to encourage an instrumental approach, meaning that the individual works for the money and attaches little importance to either intrinsic job satisfactions or the quality of social relationships encountered in the workplace. Comparably, on the new housing estates in a modern town whose industries have attracted a substantially migrant labour force, unlike in London's East End and Liverpool's 'Ship Street',[13] localised and close-knit extended family units were not in evidence and likewise, casual neighbourliness was conspicuous mainly by its absence. Life centred around home, family and television, with little involvement in any real 'community', and the resultant privatised family living helped to reinforce an instrumental orientation not only towards work itself but also towards traditional working class institutions including trade unions and the Labour Party.

Most of the affluent workers studied were both trade unionists and Labour voters, but only exceptionally did this appear to result from any strong feelings of class loyalty and solidarity. Motivations were instrumental. Workers joined the union and voted Labour for pragmatic reasons; as means towards enhancing their own private interests. Furthermore, when their images of society were probed it was most common for these privatised, instrumentally oriented workers to locate themselves in a large central stratum, distinguished at one extreme from the very rich and powerful, and at the other from 'the poor', old age pensioners, people on low pay and other residual elements. The central stratum in which respondents felt they belonged was sometimes described as the middle and sometimes as the working class but the label itself appeared unimportant. They felt no solidaristic attachment to any class. The crucial point was their tendency to see themselves as part of a mass of privatised families differentiated not in terms of basic interests and ideology but simply in terms of material possessions. Hence the investigators coin the phrase 'money model' to describe this brand of 'pecuniary' imagery subscribed to by 'commodity conscious' workers.[14]

So an alternative scenario to embourgeoisement is offered. Rather than manual workers being gradually absorbed into the middle class we are entertained to the prospect of traditional working class cultures being replaced by new, non-traditional varieties. It is necessary to point out that Lockwood offers his deferential, proletarian and privatised workers as strictly sociological rather than precisely historically situated types. There is no implication that at some point in the past all manual workers subscribed to a traditional type of imagery, nor that in the future the entire working class will become privatised. Nevertheless, the emphasis upon the prototypicality of the Luton sample indicates what is taken to be the main historical trend, for Lockwood believes that deferential and proletarian workers are concentrated in 'industries and communities which, to an ever increasing extent, are backwaters of national industrial and urban development'.[15] Hence the argument that workers will remain working class, assimilation with the white-collar strata being probable only in so far as sections of the latter are subject to proletarianisation, but the envisaged working class differs from the social formations to which the term has previously been applied.

Gavin Mackenzie's inferences from his study of skilled craftsmen on Rhode Island,[16] who were amongst the most highly paid manual workers in America, are comparable though not identical to the conclusions drawn in *The Affluent Worker*. As in Luton, the Rhode Island evidence was inconsistent with the embourgeoisement thesis but, also as in Luton, in terms of life-styles and parental aspirations, for example, contrasts with more traditional sections of the working class were evident. MacKenzie's detailed conclusions about the separation of an 'aristocracy of labour' from the rest of the manual strata cannot be neatly transposed onto the Luton study, but in each case the suggestion is that the main historical trend is not towards embourgeoisement but towards change and greater differentiation within what has formerly been a more homogeneous working class.

One point that these forecasts of a new working class share in common with the embourgeoisement thesis concerns the ease with which political implications follow. In particular, distinguishing between proletarian, deferential and privatised workers offers an alternative explanation as to why some manual workers should support a middle class political party. The deferential traditionalist, symbolised by the cap-doffing villager, can obviously be expected to offer political allegiance to his betters and, in addition to this, political analysts have been quick to identify a more pragmatic or meritocratic type of deferential voter who looks for political leadership to those better educated and qualified than himself, not because he respects their natural and ascribed right to govern, but simply because on the basis of their proven achievements he believes that they are the most competent rulers.[17] According to one school of thought this type of deference, allegiance or civility is a pervasive feature of Britain's national political culture and helps to explain why even voters who support a working class party often prefer its leaders to be middle class.[18] How this deference is sustained is an issue shrouded by debate and some writers have not been content merely to note that it is part of the political culture but have sought to identify how its cultivation has been deliberately encouraged by dominant classes whose interests it ultimately serves.[19] However, it is not difficult to see how the privatisation of working class life and a related growth of instrumental attitudes towards trade unions and politics could assist the creation of a new type of working class floating voter who feels no spontaneous loyalty to a working class party but is prepared to defer to middle class leadership if he is encouraged to feel that this will best safeguard his private interests.

Only one working class

a) *The deferential worker:* Since Lockwood's typology first appeared, interested sociologists have engaged in an extensive search for the deferential worker, the one common feature of these attempts being their failure to locate this animal in his prescribed habitat. Agricultural workers' attitudes and positions in the class structure have attracted attention out of proportion to their numerical importance, but consistent with the manner in which they offer a strategic case with which to appraise Lockwood's more general theory concerning variations in working class images of society. Labourers employed on small farms, living in small settlements and enjoying plenty of face-to-face contact with their betters have not been difficult to locate, but in parts of north-east Scotland during the period for which Carter has assembled evidence,[20] farmers seem to have been accorded deference only if they treated their workers fairly, for in other circumstances there were indications of farm-workers adopting a militant stance on 'industrial relations' issues. Newby's fieldwork in East Anglia was equally fruitless in uncovering the deferential worker.[21] Indeed, Newby found more examples of proletarian than deferential imagery amongst his farm-workers, and concluded that deference is best treated not as a quality possessed by particular individuals but as an attribute of certain types of social relationships and situations. Individuals may behave deferentially, possibly with tongue-in-cheek, in situations where their ends are served by doing so, but without necessarily adopting deferential positions across a spectrum of social and political issues and, as we shall see, this is a conclusion to which the results of our own enquiry point.

Employees in small-scale enterprises working under the ethos of small-town capitalism have also been investigated but with no greater success in locating the deferential worker. Upon the basis of data collected in Banbury, Batstone argues that such workers may be less class aware but are not more deferential than employees in large-scale industry.[22] When responding to Newby's questioning, the class images of as many as 43 per cent of the farm-workers studied proved ambivalent, meaning that they corresponded to no coherent type, and this finding is echoed in the final report of the Banbury study; 'When specific attempts were made to tap the social images which Banbury people had in their minds, weak and confused conceptions of social class emerged.'[23] As we shall see, our own findings also support the introduction of these notions of ambivalence and degrees of class awareness as more helpful in understanding variations in working class images of society than the concept of deference.

In our investigation we operationally defined deference as accepting the legitimacy of existing class differences and displaying respectful attitudes towards superordinate strata. Respondents were questioned about their attitudes towards members of whatever classes they located above their own and expressions of emulative feelings and admiration were noted, while further questions probed whether informants considered the existence of class differences to be desirable or undesirable and inevitable or avoidable. Some manual workers' answers were inevitably more deferential than others; matters could hardly have proved otherwise. But in assessing whether the deferential worker is a useful concept this is not the point at issue. Some manual workers follow soccer while others prefer rugby but this alone does not justify typifying working class images of society according to the sporting preferences involved. The crucial issue concerns whether deference is a part of a broader working class image of society associated with a coherent set of social and political values.

Our interviews involved examining fourteen separable aspects of respondents' images of class and the resultant answers were found to cluster along two separate dimensions. The first of these concerned individuals' cognitive impressions of the shape of the class structure. The number of classes that individuals recognised, the names they used to identify their own and adjacent classes, and the positions in the hierarchy where they located both their own and the largest class, comprised an inter-related cluster of items enabling a number of images of the class structure to be distinguished. Three varieties of middle class imagery were discerned, the differences amongst which are not crucial at this point save to note that the most common was not the prestige imagery sometimes considered typical of the middle class but one in which the middle class was defined as the largest and centrally positioned stratum in the social structure. As will be argued below, therefore, if manual workers place themselves in such a broad central stratum and call themselves middle class, as was the case with a proportion of the informants in *The Affluent Worker* study, there seems no good reason to deny that their images of society are bourgeois.

Two working class images were distinguishable, the first of which is labelled 'proletarian' since it contains the main features in respect of which this term has conventionally been applied. Proletarian respondents described themselves as working class, considered this class to be the largest and located it at the foot of the social scale. In these respects they saw society in 'us–them' terms, the 'us' being the subordinate group encompassing the mass of ordinary people. The only other type of working class imagery that could be distinguished, and in this case 'type' may be too strong a term, covered respondents who described themselves as working class but positioned this class towards the centre of the social hierarchy. The main features of these types of working class imagery are summarised in Table 3:1. At this stage in the discussion the key observation is that neither of these working class images proved emphatically defer-

Table 3 : 1
Working class images

	Name of own class	No. of classes recognised	Position of own class	Largest class	Position of largest class
a) *Proletarian*	Working	2	Bottom	Own	Bottom
b) *Central working class*	Working	3 or more	Centre	Own	Centre

ential. Some deferential answers to the relevant questions were offered by both proletarians and by respondents who placed themselves in a central working class, but not to the extent that would have justified labelling either as deferential images of society and rather than being distinguishable from other deferential workers, the proletarians proved if anything slightly the more deferential of the two types discerned (see Table 3 : 2).

The second dimension along which responses to the class imagery questions clustered comprised a series of items listed in Table 3 : 3, dealing not with cognitive impressions of the shape of the class structure but with affective orientations. This affective dimension incorporated

Table 3 : 2
Cognitive images and other subjective definitions of social class

	Proletarian n = 78	Central working class n = 34
Attitudes towards class above own		
a) % who definitely 'wish to be like' such people	28	24
b) % who definitely 'admire' such people	39	33
Views on class divisions		
a) % who view as 'desirable'	51	53
b) % who regard them as 'inevitable'	87	77
Views on the 'determinants' of class		
% naming 'Wealth and property'	36	46
% naming 'Power'	3	3
% naming 'Occupation'	18	12
% naming 'Income'	21	9
% naming 'How people live'	5	9
% naming 'Birth'	14	18
% naming 'Education'	1	3
% naming 'Other' determinants	3	—

Note: More than one 'determinant' might be given by each respondent.

answers to the questions designed to tap deference, namely, individuals' attitudes towards members of superordinate classes and their views on whether class differences were inevitable and desirable; but it also included respondents' attitudes to the classes they defined as lying beneath their own and their assessments of the possibility and desirability of upward social mobility. The correlates of this cluster of items will be examined in greater detail in the next chapter. For the moment it is sufficient to note that deference and its associated orientations were not properties distinctive of any broader working

Table 3:3
Affective aspects of class imagery

	Respondents stating that they both 'admired' and 'wished they were like' members of the class above their own n = 106	Respondents stating that they neither 'admired' nor 'wished they were like' members of the class above their own n = 186
Percentages who		
a) 'Admired' members of the class beneath their own	32	18
b) Would have preferred to be in the class above	68	19
c) Expected to move into a higher class	29	17
d) Regarded the existence of class differences as 'desirable'	65	47
e) Regarded the existence of class differences as 'inevitable'	90	84

class image of society. Nor, contrary to Lockwood's suggestions, was deference especially prevalent amongst workers in smaller firms or where contact with white-collar employees in the work situation was relatively extensive. As evident from Table 3:4, only three out of the eight relevant tabulations run in the predicted directions and in these cases the differences are not dramatic. It must be emphasised that we are not seeking to deny that some manual workers display more deference than others. The point being argued is that despite deliberately looking we were unable to distinguish a coherent deferential working class image of society in the sense that a proletarian image could be identified. As Newby infers, our evidence, more of which will be presented below, suggests that deference is best treated as an attribute associated with particular types of situations rather than as a pervasive quality intrinsic to certain workers' images of society.

b) *The privatised worker:* Attempts to identify the privatised worker met a similar fate to our pursuit of his deferential counterpart. Previous evidence that manual workers whose social circumstances are privatised subscribe to a pecuniary brand of imagery has been confined to *The Affluent Worker* study and one member of the research team responsible for this enquiry has subsequently shown that parts of the relevant evidence are ambiguous and susceptible to alternative interpretations.[24] For the purposes of our enquiry privatisation was defined and measured in terms of the number of friends

Table 3:4

Work situation and social class attitudes of blue-collar respondents

	Size of firm		Amount of contact reported with white-collar employees at work	
	Small[1] n = 89	Large n = 136	Considerable/ frequent n = 112	None at all n = 27
Attitudes towards class above own				
a) % emulative	24	28	27	23
b) % admire	37	41	38	39
Consider the existence of classes				
a) % desirable	60	51	45	77
b) % inevitable	86	81	83	84

[1] Small = less than 100 employees.

respondents reported at work and amongst their neighbours and by these criteria we distinguished a relatively privatised section of our manual sample. Our main interest, needless to say, lay not in demonstrating the existence of such individuals which could not be seriously doubted, but in determining whether they subscribed to a special type of class imagery distinguished by its pecuniary character.

To test this issue we examined whether privatised respondents tended to locate themselves in a large central stratum, as hypothesised in *The Affluent Worker*, and also invited respondents to name the determinants of individuals' class positions, our interest being in whether privatised informants would prove exceptionally likely to mention income. The results presented in Table 3 : 5 lend some support to the hypotheses being tested in so far as three out of the four relevant tabulations run in the predicted directions. However, these results also show that, although more likely to do so than others, the majority of privatised respondents did not place themselves in a large, centrally positioned class. In the relevant columns in Table 3:5 the highest proportion giving 'money model' answers is 34 per cent. Similarly, although they were marginally more likely to mention income than others, the majority of the privatised respondents did not name this as a determinant of individuals' class positions and collectively they mentioned a wide range of additional factors as was the case amongst every other sub-section of the sample. Even amongst individuals who are agreed upon the shape of the class structure, there is little consensus about the factors that determine

Table 3:5

Privatisation and perceptions of social class of blue-collar respondents

	Number of 'close friends' at work		Number of 'friends' amongst neighbours	
	2 and under n = 134	3 or more n = 27	None n = 65	3 or more n = 59
% place selves in large central stratum	34	25	28	28
% name 'income' as a determinant of class position	22	16	28	16

a person's class position. In the real world, as Table 3 : 2 illustrates, proletarian images of society do not always stress power as the main difference between classes, nor do privatised workers always attach supreme importance to income.

Our results, therefore, do not suggest that pecuniary orientations are best regarded as the basis for a distinct type of working class imagery. As was the case with deference, in some respects proletarian workers' responses actually proved more pecuniary than those of manual workers who subscribed to a different type of working class imagery (see Table 3 : 2). It seems preferable to treat pecuniary orientations as tendencies that can occur in varying degrees within other more general images of society and that are encouraged by privatised circumstances but which are never sufficiently prominent to result in a separate type of imagery.

c) *The proletarian worker:* In contrast with the deferential and privatised varieties, our endeavours to identify a proletarian type of

worker produced positive results. Indeed, the concept of the proletarian worker did all that could be asked of a sociological type. As
already indicated, from the questions tapping respondents' images
of class the proletarian was one of the two working class images of
society that could be discerned. In addition to this, the proletarian
concept also 'worked' in proving related to the views that respondents expressed across a range of social and political issues. A proletarian image of society was related to the adoption of a radical or
left-wing posture on virtually every issue explored. Workers who
subscribed to proletarian imagery were more likely than any other

Table 3:6

Blue-collar class images and socio-political attitudes

		Class image	
	Proletarian n = 78	Central working class n = 34	Middle class n = 61
% voted Conservative at previous general election	19	32	39
% in favour of more nationalisation	42	21	36
% approve of Enoch Powell's views on immigration and race relations	61	71	75
% approve of 'Women's Lib'	21	9	13
% unqualified approval of married women working	32	24	21
% support for the re-introduction of capital punishment	81	88	92
% in favour of trade unions aiming to 'increase workers' share'	26	27	17
% agree that trade unions have too much power	27	59	64

section of the manual sample to vote Labour, favour further nationalisation, argue that trade unions have too little power, disapprove
of Enoch Powell's views on immigration and race relations, oppose
the re-introduction of capital punishment and to approve of
'Women's Lib' in general and married women working in particular
(see Table 3:6). As the use of the concept has conventionally implied,
a proletarian image of society is related to a broader set of oppositional values; oppositional not only in the sense of usually favouring some change in the status quo, but more importantly in that every
case quoted involved the proletarians being the manual group most
likely to dissent from the majority position endorsed throughout the
entire sample.

Some of these qualities of the proletarian worker, especially his liberal attitudes towards race relations, Women's Lib and capital punishment, may seem inconsistent with what are commonly regarded as working class values. To avoid any misleading impressions, therefore, we must point out that on aggregate manual respondents were *less* likely than white-collar informants to adopt liberal positions on each of the above issues. Furthermore, as the figures in Table 3:6 demonstrate, the views of the typical proletarian worker

Table 3:7

Blue-collar class images and related factors

		Class image	
	Proletarian n = 78	Central working class n = 34	Middle class n = 61
	%	%	%
'Close friends' at work			
None	41	53	52
1 or 2	19	24	30
3 or more	40	24	18
Trade union members	79	62	72
Father's occupational status:			
White-collar	9	16	20
Type of housing			
Owner-occupier	18	32	51
Council tenant	71	47	39
'Friends' amongst neighbours			
None	31	50	31
1 or 2	37	24	39
3 or more	32	26	30

were in no sense liberal. The situation was rather that the views of manual respondents who subscribed to proletarian imagery were somewhat less illiberal than in any other section of the blue-collar sample.

In addition to being distinguished by their oppositional values, respondents with proletarian images of the class structure turned out to be clustered in exactly the types of circumstances suggested in previous analyses (see Table 3:7). Compared with other blue-collar informants, the proletarians were exceptionally strongly integrated into occupational communities assessed in terms of the number of close friends reported, density of trade union membership was higher than amongst other groups, the proportion with blue-collar parents was also higher, while their homes were exceptionally likely to be situated on council housing estates. The feature common to each of these circumstances is the implication of the individual standing immersed in a blue-collar social network. Amongst our proletarian respondents, social relationships with other blue-collar workers were unusually extensive while contacts with the world of the white-collar worker were inconspicuous. This type of encapsulation within blue-collar social networks based both within and outside the workplace favours the development of a distinctly proletarian image of society. The concept of the proletarian worker highlights processes very much in operation in the real world. In drawing attention to an image of society bearing a genuine resemblance to ideas situated in individuals' minds, the concept enables meaningful connections to be traced between the circumstances amidst which many blue-collar workers live and their socio-political responses.

d) *The central working class:* Although derived from survey data, the notion of a central working class proves less satisfactory as an ideal type than the proletarian model, meaning that it fails to clarify the same range of phenomena. Some members of our blue-collar sample's answers to the class imagery questions certainly clustered into a distinguishable group with individuals identifying themselves as working class but locating this stratum towards the centre rather than at the base of the social hierarchy. However, unlike the proletarian model, the presence of central working class imagery was not associated with any obviously coherent pattern of responses to the questions dealing with socio-political issues (see Table 3 : 6). There was no general tendency that could be called deferential, pecuniary or summarised beneath any equally convenient label. Rather than representing an alternative working class ideology, central working class responses were simply less consistently oppositional than those co-existing alongside proletarian images of society. The socio-political dispositions of this group, therefore, appear best regarded not as a separate type but just less working class in character than those of the proletarians.

In terms of certain social indicators, the profiles of central working class informants were similar or veered towards those of manual workers who described themselves as middle class, the cases in point concerning social class origins, immersion in occupational communities and housing circumstances (see Table 3 : 7). However, despite their inclination to locate themselves above the bottom rung of the ladder, the overall socio-economic positions of central working class informants could not be likened to an aristocracy of labour. They are not particularly affluent, comprising 19 per cent of blue-collar respondents earning less than £2000 per year but only 8 per cent of the more highly paid, and members of this central working class were similarly biased towards semi- and unskilled rather than skilled manual occupations. Rather than a blue-collar élite, these members of the sample are better portrayed as a peripheral working class whose immersion in blue-collar social relationships and situations was relatively weak. As evident in Table 3:7, they were more likely than any other group of blue-collar respondents to remain outside the trade union movement and to report no friendship attachments into neighbourhood communities.

In our view, therefore, it seems unwise to treat this central working class as equivalent to the proletarian image of society harbouring an alternative working class meaning system and arising amidst a distinctive configuration of working class circumstances. The circumstances of this group appear better regarded as just working class but rather less 'solidly' so than the situations associated with proletarian imagery, and similarly, their attitudes and class identities appear most appropriately treated as simply working class but without such a sharp degree of class awareness as exhibited in proletarian imagery.

Lockwood's typology along with Elizabeth Bott's earlier work on class ideologies has enjoyed considerable influence during the last decade and, apart from the substantive arguments which have been considered above, their general contribution to debates about class awareness has involved fashioning a localised idiom by drawing attention to the importance of the individual's immediate environment. The underlying argument behind the notions of deferential workers, privatised workers, power models and prestige imagery, suggests that people do not perceive their society as would a detached observer but that individuals are most aware of and responsive to the social relationships in which they are immediately involved.

These insights have undoubtedly been useful and have enlightened long-standing debates in sociology, such as why manual workers do not always become conscious of how their collective interests conflict with those of capital. However, whilst recognising this contribution, there may be dangers in entirely surrendering the study of class awareness to unravelling the implications of various groups' local environments. Indeed, there has remained a contrary school of thought which has accused the focusing of attention upon the implications of workplace, neighbourhood relations and other such microcosmic features of manual workers' circumstances, of obscuring the societal role of the working class and its potential historical significance. Notwithstanding the relevance of their immediate situations, it may be unsafe to assume that manual workers, or any other group, are totally unaware of and insensitive to the macro-scheme of inequalities and that they are completely uninfluenced by broader ideological currents.

Even if, as some writers have suggested, the working class is unable to generate a truly revolutionary consciousness from within itself and will be converted to socialism only with outside assistance,[25] simply being a manual worker with all that this implies for income and career patterns and treatment in the work situation can hardly fail to dispose individuals towards a proletarian view of their places in society and an associated set of oppositional values. Given this general working class situation, then local circumstances may either play or fail to play a consolidating role. Local milieux that protect and encapsulate blue-collar employees in working class social relationships at work, amongst neighbours and in trade unions can consolidate working class opposition into a sharply proletarian outlook.[26] Other circumstances, however, do not result in different types of working class, but just less class aware workers. Following this necessary but complex examination of previously postulated working class images and situations, therefore, there remains simply one working class to feature in subsequent chapters.

The bourgeois manual worker

If our enquiry confirms the authenticity of the proletarian worker, it equally argues for the resurrection of the bourgeois manual worker as a sociological type. Despite being conducted on 'militant Merseyside', our survey located many manual workers, approximately a quarter of those interviewed, who subscribed to middle class images of society. Of course, the fact that some manual workers align themselves with the middle class is well known and acknowledged in the relevant literature, and the existence of middle class identifiers within our blue-collar sample in no sense rates as an unexpected discovery. However, there has been a tendency to try to 'explain away' this deviant blue-collar minority. For example, some writers have refused to admit that their orientations are really middle class and have preferred to regard them as exceptionally deferential, status or commodity-conscious workers. The aspect of our findings that must be emphasised, therefore, is that there were no subtle differences between our manual respondents' middle class images and those presented by white-collar informants. The middle class with which some manual respondents identified was a large central stratum, for others it comprised a number of finely divided layers, whilst in further cases it was defined as a relatively small group located above a larger working class and exactly the same range of variation was evident amongst the white-collar sample.

The failure of previous studies of reputedly prototypical sections of the blue-collar labour force to discover impressive numbers of bourgeois workers can be explained in two ways. Firstly, some investigators have demanded that unrealistically tight criteria be met before admitting embourgeoisement. For example, some investigators have looked for signs of the 'prestige imagery' which ever since Bott distinguished the type has often been taken as the modal form of middle class awareness. Secondly, some of the situations selected for enquiry in the quest for signs of embourgeoisement have probably been less favourable than the investigators intended. For example, the results of our survey show that the factors most conducive to bourgeois orientations amongst manual workers imply neither affluence nor residence on 'new' housing estates, nor employment in modern industries.

The circumstances favouring the presence of middle class images of society amongst manual workers are summarised in Table 3:8. The figures themselves make unavoidably heavy reading but the inferences that they support are clear and simple. Bourgeois images of society arise where manual workers are surrounded by the opposites of those circumstances which consolidate a proletarian outlook. Whereas proletarian respondents tended to have been born into blue-collar families, lived mainly on working class council estates and were knit by friendships into work-based communities, the bourgeois informants derived from white-collar origins, lived on owner-occupied and mainly middle class housing developments and were only weakly connected with occupation-based communities. Rather than shielded by a circle of blue-collar social relationships and thereby immersed in a working class culture, the bourgeois workers were exceptionally exposed to white-collar influences.

Each of the circumstances listed above was independently associated with diminishing proletarian and increasing middle class modes of awareness, but the cross-tabulations show the sharpest variations occurring alongside housing. Previous studies[27] have suggested that even if not synonymous with assimilation into the middle class, the movement of manual workers into owner-occupied suburbs is related to a marked shift in the direction of middle class attitudes and life-styles and our findings confirm this impression. This potency

Table 3:8

Blue-collar class images, housing, social origins and occupational community

Type of class imagery	Owner-occupier		Council house tenant	
	None or one close friend at work n = 48	Two or more close friends at work n = 25	None or one close friend at work n = 60	Two or more close friends at work n = 55
	%	%	%	%
Proletarian	17	24	42	55
Central working class	15	16	18	9
Middle class	52	24	18	24
Other	17	36	22	13

Type of class imagery	Father's occupation: White-collar		Father's occupation: Blue-collar	
	None or one close friend at work n = 25	Two or more close friends at work n = 10	None or one close friend at work n = 99	Two or more close friends at work n = 74
	%	%	%	%
Proletarian	20	20	31	49
Central working class	16	10	18	12
Middle class	32	40	32	20
Other	32	30	18	19

Type of class imagery	Father's occupation: White-collar		Father's occupation: Blue-collar	
	Owner-occupiers n = 14	Council house tenants n = 14	Owner-occupiers n = 57	Council house tenants n = 97
	%	%	%	%
Proletarian	14	36	19	51
Central working class	7	7	18	16
Middle class	50	28	41	19
Other	29	29	23	14

of housing circumstances perhaps helps to explain why housing policy should be so emotive as a party political issue. Since it is the case that class images are related to party political loyalties, the Labour Party has a vested electoral interest in maintaining the predominantly blue-collar communities that can be found on council estates, whilst the Conservative Party has an equivalent interest in the spread of home-ownership.

When analysing survey data it is informative to isolate the significance of independent factors. However, it is important to remember that in the real world discrete variables never operate in splendid isolation. Amongst our manual sample, the circumstances named above as associated with the presence of middle class imagery all proved related to one another (see Table 3:9). Manual respondents with white-collar fathers were more likely than other blue-collar workers to be owner-occupiers and were less likely to be closely in-

Table 3:9

Blue-collar social origins, housing and occupational community

Father's occupation	Owner-occupier n = 77	Council house tenant n = 120
	%	%
White-collar	21	12
Blue-collar	79	88

Close friends at work	Owner-occupier n = 77	Council house tenant n = 120
	%	%
None or one	65	53
Two or more	35	47

	Close friends at work	
Father's occupation	None or one n = 129	Two or more n = 89
	%	%
White-collar	19	14
Blue-collar	81	86

tegrated into occupational communities. Hence we have identified not just a list of factors but a syndrome of circumstances that tend to occur not singly but in a combination amidst which manual workers are likely to adopt middle class images of society.

Education and affluence also played a part in consolidating middle class imagery, but not as powerful a role as in the case of the circumstances mentioned above. The relevant figures are presented in Table 3:10 and the inferences are straightforward. When the prime circumstances are favourable, an above average income and an education beyond the compulsory minimum increase the likelihood of manual workers adopting middle class images. On the other hand, when circumstances otherwise favour a proletarian outlook, education and affluence have no such association. Whereas white-collar origins, home-ownership and a lack of involvement in communal relationships at work are primary influences, income and education play only secondary, consolidating roles in the development of middle class outlooks amongst manual workers.

For anyone suspecting that our manual respondents who identified with a middle class were not really bourgeois, their social and political attitudes offer an adequate reply. Middle class imagery amongst manual workers is associated with all that are conventionally recognised as middle class values. In terms of party political

Table 3:10
Blue-collar class images, education and income

Type of class imagery	Left school at 14 or 15/No further education n = 119	Left school at 16 or older/Some further education n = 27
	%	%
Proletarian	38	37
Central working class	20	4
Middle class	21	41
Other	21	19
	Up to £2000 p.a. n = 145	Over £2000 p.a. n = 61
	%	%
Proletarian	37	33
Central working class	19	8
Middle class	24	39
Other	20	20

loyalties, attitudes towards trade unions and the other semi-political issues about which the sample was questioned, bourgeois manual respondents' answers were consistently skewed away from the proletarian and towards the typical white-collar position. And when manual respondents were surrounded by all the main circumstances conducive to bourgeois imagery, as the figures in Table 3 : 11 indicate, their socio-political attitudes were not merely 'tainted' with middle class tendencies but were virtually indistinguishable from those of the white-collar sample as a whole.

The bourgeois worker is as effective as the proletarian as a sociological type. Both types are equally useful in enabling meaningful connections to be established between the circumstances amidst which different sections of the blue-collar labour force live, their images of society and their socio-political orientations. Irrespective of whether the historical trend is towards embourgeoisement, the bourgeois worker is a very living animal and there are grounds for caution before dismissing his mode of awareness as false or arguing that he is not a 'real' representative of the blue-collar labour force. The circumstances associated with bourgeois orientations are in no sense inconsistent with the demands of manual employment and

Table 3:11
Proletarian and bourgeois blue-collar workers

	Blue-collar workers		White-collar workers
	Blue-collar father Council house tenants Two or more 'close friends' at work n = 49	White-collar fathers Owner-occupiers Less than two 'close friends' at work n = 11	n = 243
	%	%	%
Images of class			
Proletarian	57	18	14
Central working class	11	9	11
Middle class	19	54	61
Other	13	18	14
Voted Conservative at last election	15	67	72
In favour of extension of nationalisation	50	36	24
Support trade unions aiming to 'increase workers' share'	37	11	14
Agree that trade unions have 'too much power'	35	73	66

before labelling any types of awareness as false it is advisable to remember that all forms of consciousness are developed within given systems of social relationships and in the context of prevailing ideas, and contacts with bourgeois influences are no less authentic aspects of manual workers' milieux than associations with other blue-collar workers.

From the evidence reviewed, therefore, two major dimensions of variation are apparent in manual workers' images of society and related socio-political attitudes. Firstly there is a 'vertical' dimension along which proletarian and bourgeois orientations are located at opposite ends and it is necessary to stress that this dimension is a continuum. It is not an either/or case in which all manual workers can be unambiguously categorised in one group or the other. As a result of exposure to cross-pressures, various midway positions can occur. Then there is a quite separate dimension of variation. At the bourgeois end of the first continuum there are several types of middle class imagery, detailed distinctions between which will be charted in subsequent chapters, towards any of which bourgeois manual workers may approximate. At the proletarian end of the scale, this radical and oppositional mode of awareness varies in its degrees of precision. Hence it is entirely possible for proletarian awareness to weaken without manual workers' perspectives becoming bourgeois. These are the dimensions along which variations occur and questions regarding the direction of historical change are best examined within the framework that these dimensions offer.

Embourgeoisement: a re-assessment

If we have resurrected the bourgeois worker, it by no means follows that the embourgeoisement thesis deserves a revival. Mackenzie has noted the difficulties that confront all attempts to infer historical trends from cross-sectional evidence. While arguing the existence of an aristocracy of labour and inferring that the class structure in America is becoming more rather than less complex, he acknowledges the difference between inference and proof. 'Whether this situation is different from that existing previously or only from that *perceived* to have existed earlier, I am not able to prove.'[28] Unfortunately, cross-sectional evidence is necessarily our main source material since we cannot refer to national surveys conducted in the past that collected all the information that we would now like to have available. As a result, declarations about the direction of change cannot be more than best-guess exercises. The task can be made to look easier if we work from simple notions about the past condition of the working class. If we imagine that there was once a dark or golden age of revolutionary solidarity it becomes easy to note how different things have now become. But despite any superficial appeal, substituting guess-work for history cannot add confidence to inferences concerning the direction of change.

We can read the speeches of actual and would-have-been labour leaders but in truth little is reliably known about ordinary working-class attitudes in nineteenth and early twentieth-century Britain. However, the evidence available from historical research indicates that the range of variation in present-day manual workers' attitudes is anything but novel. The most cursory acquaintance with the historical record makes it clear that there is little sense in postulating any one type of traditional working-class. The embourgoisement debate is not new but has been sometimes live and meantimes flickering for over a hundred years. Commentators have constantly been aware of bourgeois elements in the manual labour force. In the nineteenth century an aristocracy of labour with skill in its hands was clearly distinguishable and considered itself distinct from the likes of railway navvies—itinerant workers who tramped from job to job, socially disorganised and living in temporary shacks with sexual unions rarely solemnised, with nothing but labour, crude muscle power, to sell.[29] The terms 'blue-collar' and 'manual' have passed into common currency during the twentieth century, partly at the expense of older expressions such as craftsman, artisan and labourer that give some indication of the heterogeneity that reigned amongst nineteenth-century working-men. The 'respectable' could be set against the 'roughs' and, in addition, the industrial revolution nurtured class conscious workers. Foster has shown that in certain industrial towns, including Oldham, a radical working class consciousness began to crystallise during the first half of the nineteenth century, although in other places, including South Shields and Northampton, about which information was also collected, no comparable developments were apparent.[30] The evidence assembled by Clayre on attitudes towards work and leisure in the nineteenth century shows that we can dismiss all suspicion that the instrumentally orientated worker might be a twentieth-century novelty.[31] The industrial revolution created its own boom towns, including the Durham pit villages during that period—mini-Lutons that attracted migrant workers presumably intent upon maximising their earnings.[32]

If we wish to discuss the possible future, rather than estimating and extrapolating the gross direction of past change, there is greater merit in taking stock of the present situation that we can know in greater depth and assessing into what it is likely to develop, and one best-guess we will hazard concerns the unlikelihood of embourgeoisement being a contemporary trend that will shortly overwhelm the working class. There are three reasons for suspecting that although bourgeois workers certainly exist it is unlikely that they will become increasingly representative of the manual strata. The first is that although our evidence portrays the bourgeois worker as a living animal, the data also indicate that he is not easily bred. Whilst a number of factors favour the development of middle class attitudes amongst manual workers, none is sufficiently powerful, in isolation, to guarantee a bourgeois outcome. The appearance of middle class attitudes only becomes even probable when a constellation of favourable circumstances coincide and although these circumstances are mutually inter-related and occur together more frequently than would be expected by chance, their intersection remains rare. In our sample totalling 231 manual workers, there were only eleven cases where all the prime circumstances favouring the appearance of bourgeois attitudes intersected; that is, where the subject was an owner-occupier, reported no more than a single close friend at work and whose father held a white-collar job.

Second, while some of the circumstances related to the presence of middle class imagery amongst manual workers are likely to become more widespread, the cases in point being home-ownership, affluence and education in excess of the statutory minimum, there are no grounds for believing that other favourable circumstances are destined to become increasingly common. There are no indications, for example, that downward inter-generational mobility into the blue-collar strata is on the increase. It is mistaken to assume that bourgeois blue-collar workers must be located in particularly 'advanced' sections of the labour force whose circumstances are destined to become increasingly typical.

The third reason for doubting the likelihood of embourgeoisement overwhelming the working class is that, although our evidence implies that it can happen to individual workers, the data also indicate that as a collective phenomenon embourgeoisement is a self-arresting process. Our evidence suggests that at any given point in time embourgeoisement can affect only minority sections of the manual strata. Several writers have drawn attention to how individuals' attitudes and reactions to their income levels depend upon their reference groups. Hence the reaction of workers earning £2000 per year will be different when this is a mainly middle class privilege, as at the time of our enquiry, than when it has become low pay even when judged against manual standards. Similarly the implications of home-ownership can be expected to change if and when it becomes increasingly common and likewise with an extended education. If the circumstances currently associated with the development of middle class attitudes amongst manual workers did become more widespread, this alone could be sufficient to alter their implications.

It is interesting to re-scrutinise the reports of surveys conducted during the nineteen-fifties when observers were noting how the middle class ethos surrounding the new council estates that were then appearing encouraged residents to feel a cut above the traditional working-class.[33] If the results of our enquiry are any guide, by the nineteen-seventies the council estate has lost all bourgeois associations and has become especially hospitable to a proletarian culture. Circumstances that once symbolised middle class status and were the privileges of 'advanced' sections of the working class can rapidly acquire proletarian connotations. All that is required is their extension to the majority of manual workers.

An atmosphere of drama is lent to its discussion if an impression is created of the working class standing on the verge of some major transformation. Hence the common practice of investigators seeking out apparently advanced sections of the manual strata in order to offer a glimpse of things to come. So if not embourgeoisement, then what? Maybe we should keep this dramatic idiom at arm's length for in the immediate future the working class may remain little different compared with the recent past.

There has always been variety and also change within the working-class, but the on-going currents of change have never operated with exactly the same effect throughout all sections of the blue-collar labour force. Technological change, for example, has been a constant feature of economic life since the industrial revolution but has never wrought identical consequences upon all occupations. In some industries recent technological 'progress' has left the man on the monotonous assembly-line with little scope for anything but an instrumental approach to work that offers few intrinsic satisfactions. Elsewhere, in contrast, technological advance has meant automated continuous-process plants which, according to one school of thought, replace alienation with freedom.[34] There is always scope for investigators to argue about whose sample should be considered genuinely prototypical. In the motor industry conditions unfavourable to solidaristic occupational communities may have been undermining traditional forms of proletarian consciousness but there are other industries, including hotels and catering, where organisational and technical trends favour proletarianisation. There is merit in Chivers's suggestion that 'researchers might usefully bear in mind that they should look not only for trends away from working class consciousness but for trends towards it too'.[35]

The net pattern of change in the working class is as likely to be subtle as dramatic and it is sensible to resist temptations to exaggerate trends that may be temporary or confined to certain sections of the manual strata. Given these qualifications, our best guess is that the net trends are not so much away from proletarian and towards bourgeois forms of consciousness as away from sharply oppositional proletarianism and towards a relatively dissipated (though not necessarily less militant) class awareness.

There are a number of on-going trends the net effects of which are liable to erode formerly encapsulated blue-collar social networks and undermine the proletarian awareness that we have shown to be associated with this type of milieu. If the pace of economic and technological change is accelerating and affecting rates of labour mobility accordingly, then although workplace mateyness is unlikely to be eradicated, the maintenance of solidaristic occupational communities must become increasingly difficult. Similarly, the massive programmes of re-housing in which many longer-standing inner-urban working class communities are disappearing may be laying the foundation for comparable though rarely quite as closely knit communities on new council estates, but the drift from the city centres is also leading to a growth of owner-occupied suburbs. Over a period of generations the course of educational change is unlikely to be without similar effect. For all the talk of neighbourhood comprehensives limiting the horizons of working class children, they hardly compare with the local elementary and secondary modern schools that have been successively replaced. Likewise the long-term influence of the mass media can hardly do other than contribute to breaking the cultural barriers that formerly enclosed working class communities.

Forecasting inevitably involves some speculation, but by eliminating the improbable our confidence that the remaining alternatives are possible can increase and on this basis we anticipate not a bourgeois labour force but less community in the traditional sense and, therefore, less proletarian solidarity with blue-collar opposition becoming less focused within the only coherent working class ideology available. The signs of this trend provide our first encounter with the fragmentary class structure, a theme that links patterns of change that are occurring not only within the working class but also at other levels in the social hierarchy.

4. Working Class Mobility Orientations and Education

Education and life-chances

Interest in the directions of social change affecting the working class co-exists alongside an equivalent concern to understand more enduring aspects of working class life. Amongst these is the lack of educational success experienced by working class children and, therefore, the persistence of inequalities of opportunity.

In most societies the role of the family in social placement has been uncontroversial. Throughout history son following father has normally been regarded as a proper arrangement. In modern societies, however, contrary values have become prevalent. The dominant presumption now favours equality, meaning that inequalities are considered unacceptable unless justified either in terms of their contributions to the commonwealth or by reference to the exceptional merits of the beneficiaries and one example is the virtually unchallenged view that individuals should be allocated amongst positions that are unequally rewarded according to their own achievements rather than by 'accident' of birth. Yet the family remains the institution within which not only procreation but also the care and socialisation of children normally occur and the positions at which individuals first enter the class structure, therefore, inevitably depend upon to whom they are born.

Outside the hippie fringe and its predecessors, alternatives to the family have never been widely canvassed. Education has been chosen as the means of reconciling the role of the family with the desire to create equality of opportunity. Since the nineteenth century, occupational and thereby more general social placement has become increasingly dependent upon educational success. The diploma rather than patronage and purchase of office has become the key to life-chances and ever since education began acting as a prominent apparatus of social placement, a parallel demand for equal access to educational opportunity has been growing. Entry to the secondary schools in Britain, the traditional route to higher education and advantageous job prospects, was originally by payment, but access has gradually widened. Following the 1902 Act a scholarship route was institutionalised enabling bright products of the elementary schools to proceed to free places in secondary education. Then, following the 1944 Act, all children, with the exception of approximately 5 per cent whose parents desired and could afford an independent education, were placed on an apparently equal footing with entry to the different types of secondary schools that were introduced, depending solely upon their performances in an impartial selection procedure that became known as the eleven-plus. In 1944 it was widely believed that equality of opportunity had arrived and that children's educational prospects and overall life-chances would forthwith depend entirely upon each individual's own abilities and accomplishments rather than upon the socio-economic standing of his parents.

However, it is now common knowledge that the 1944 Act failed to realise its supporters' hopes. No sooner had it been implemented than it became apparent that the Act had not established genuine equality of opportunity. Beginning in the nineteen-fifties, a series of government reports chronicled a situation in which a strong link remained between children's educational attainments and their social class origins.[1] During this same period a succession of independent investigators began exploring the processes enabling social class to exercise its pervasive influence and as a result it became evident that working class children were the more likely to fall at every hurdle in what had been intended to operate as an impartial educational competition. Social class was shown to be related to the streams into which primary school children were allocated, their success in the eleven-plus selection procedures, the streams towards which they gravitated within secondary schools, their likelihood of staying on beyond the statutory leaving age and their subsequent chances of entering higher education.

By the end of this sequence, social class disparities are extremely wide. At any one stage in the process of educational selection, social class might appear to be playing only a marginal role in distinguishing between successes and failures, but this cannot be said of its cumulative importance. While approximately two-thirds of all children in Britain come from working class families, these families supply only a quarter of all university students. In 1964 Little and Westergaard aroused consternation when they drew together the evidence showing that although the chances of children from all levels in the social scale eventually entering higher education had increased since the inter-war period, the class differential had remained virtually static[2] and more recent evidence collated by Noble suggests that any subsequent trend towards greater equality of opportunity has been no more than marginal.[3] It is because educational success is far from evenly distributed between young people from different social class origins that rates of social mobility remain far from 'perfect' and although the contemporary class structure displays nothing resembling a caste-like rigidity, few individuals move far away from the levels of social scale into which they are born.

Since the nineteen-fifties further reforms have been introduced amidst hopes of a more genuine movement towards equality of opportunity than followed the 1944 Act. Programmes of 'positive discrimination' and 'compensatory education' in favour of children and districts otherwise liable to suffer handicaps have been mounted, while its supporters have hoped that the transition to a comprehensive secondary school system might work to the net advantage of working class children. The hard evidence that has become available, however, suggests that these hopes will prove as hollow as the passionate enthusiasm of 1944.[4]

Parental attitudes

There is little argument about these basic facts of the situation, but when it comes to explaining the facts the problem becomes more confused. The explanations on offer do not even fall into a simple set of alternatives and it seems unlikely that any single theory will prove to contain the whole truth. There is debate surrounding the significance of innate differences in ability, but even those who argue the importance of hereditary factors do not claim that they explain all the variance in educational attainment between the social classes. Then there are arguments concerning the nature of social class differences in linguistic styles and their implications for educability.

This latter debate has centred largely around the theories of Basil Bernstein who originally distinguished formal or elaborated from public or restricted codes, arguing that children reared in working class milieux were the less likely to be introduced to the former and that their progress in school was consequently likely to be impaired.[5] These claims have stimulated extensive research and writing. Doubts have been expressed as to whether working and middle class uses of language can really be distinguished in the ways that Bernstein claimed and, in addition to Bernstein himself,[6] several other investigators have conducted fieldwork to clarify this issue.[7] There has been further debate concerning whether, in so far as they do possess special properties, working class linguistic styles can be meaningfully described as 'restricted' and considered impediments to educability, for an alternative view contends that working class speech is not inferior to but merely different from the middle class language that is employed in schools.[8]

Unravelling all the approaches to explaining the social class/educational attainment relationship that are on offer would be a complex task in its own right and the following discussion focuses upon just one line of argument, albeit one considered by many writers to be of basic importance. A number of investigators have identified 'parental attitudes' as a key intervening variable helping to explain the connection between children's social class origins and their educational attainments and that parental attitudes themselves are class-related is firmly established. In comparison with middle class samples, surveys have repeatedly portrayed working class parents as relatively uninterested and unencouraging. Jackson and Marsden[9] have shown how middle class parents who fear that their children may fail to obtain grammar school places will visit the school to discuss the problem, arrange special coaching if it seems desirable and, sometimes, as a last resort, opt for the expense of private education. Middle class parents want educational success for their children and are prepared to take whatever remedial or supportive action is necessary if and when obstacles arise.[10] In contrast, all the comparable evidence portrays working class parents as developing only modest aspirations and accepting signs of portending failure passively as evidence that a child does not possess the ability to make it. Mays has described the apathy that can consequently envelop the schools in a working class inner-city area, eventually encouraging uninterest on the part of teachers.[11] Working class parents are relatively easy to please and, therefore, do not provide the push that helps middle class children win through to high levels of educational achievement.

Young and McGeeney[12] describe the almost paradoxical situation in a primary school selected for study having been identified by the researchers as housing a problem of under-achievement, where interviews with the parents disclosed almost unblemished satisfaction. Most parents considered the school to be very good, offering a far better education than anything they had experienced when young, and were well satisfied with their children's progress. These parents were in no sense hostile towards education but their expectations were modest and, therefore, easily fulfilled. In addition, the prevalent feeling defined education as the school's business. Parents felt that they were not required to 'interfere' and only expected to have to go to school in the event of 'trouble'. These parents were unlikely to drive either themselves or their children neurotic with educational anxieties but, on the other hand, neither were they likely to push their children on to eventual success.

The investigations conducted on behalf of the Plowden Committee[13] confirmed previous suggestions of working class parents being relatively devoid of interest in their children's education. This Committee's enquiries confirmed that working class parents were less likely than middle class parents to have visited their children's primary schools and done all the other things that could be construed as pushing or encouraging their offspring up the educational ladder. In analysing the available evidence, the Plowden Committee concluded that parental attitudes were considerably more important than material circumstances in explaining working class children's relatively poor attainments and the types of positive discrimination advocated were largely intended to stimulate parental interest.

In order to understand the 'problem' of under-achievement amongst working class pupils, an essential point to grasp is that neither the majority of the children nor the parents directly involved are conscious of any problem. Although it is a live concern, the demand for equality of educational opportunity is not one of the emotive grass-roots issues of our time. It may be defined as such by an assortment of intellectuals with backgrounds in education, the social sciences and politics but it awakens little anger in working class communities and this is one reason why the 'problem' persists.

Mobility orientations

That parental attitudes vary as described above and that these differences are amongst the immediate causes of under-achievement on the part of working class children must be considered as established beyond dispute. However, the genesis of the parental attitudes in question and, therefore, what might be done to check their current implications, are controversial issues. One explanation as to why parental attitudes should vary along social class lines postulates a lack of symmetry between more general working class mobility orientations on the one hand and the middle class values alleged to be enshrined in mainstream educational practice on the other, as the underlying problem, and this argument interfaces with the broader issue being examined throughout these chapters, concerning the composition of working class culture, images of society and related attitudes. In previous chapters we have seen that there are important qualitative differences between working and middle class images of society and related values, and the suggestion that has arisen in educational discourse postulates that this polarisation includes mobility orientations, these being perceptions and evaluations of the possibility and desirability of individual upward social mobility. It is commonly believed that the middle classes emphasise the virtues of individual enterprise and both recognise and seek to exploit opportunities for personal advancement, while the working class adheres to a collectivist outlook, with individuals seeking to improve their circumstances only as members of the groups to which they already belong. Not only is it commonly believed but it is not difficult to find evidence to support this commonsense view. Members of the working class join trade unions to defend and enhance their mutual interests, and give their votes to a Labour Party that traditionally supports collectivist welfare measures. Elizabeth Bott's research has become a 'classical' source of support for this theory though her fieldwork covered only twenty London families.[14] Bott juxtaposed the prestige imagery of the middle classes in which the social hierarchy was regarded as a series of emulative layers inviting the individual to climb, against the power model, dichotomous, us/them imagery of the working class which allowed either fatalistic acquiescence or a quest for collective improvement but militated against any desire to join the 'other side'. In his subsequent discussion of variations in working class images of society, Lockwood endorsed this view though again on the basis of little systematically assembled empirical evidence, treating a disinclination to seek personal mobility as a feature distinguishing all working class images.[15] Once an antithesis between individual ambition and working class values is assumed, the implications for education become readily apparent.[16]

Implications of occupying different positions

Banks and Finlayson have pointed out that 'whether the lower aspirations of working class parents are part of a distinctive set of value orientations which place a low value on achievement or whether they simply reflect a process of adjustment to circumstances is, however, still very much a matter of debate'.[17] This is the crux of the problem now under discussion. It cannot be denied that working class parents do not display the same interest and ambition as regards their children's education that is evident in middle class circles. Similarly there can be no dispute that manual workers join trade unions in search of collective betterment and vote for a Labour

Party that favours collectivist welfare measures, but whether all this is because working class culture places little value upon personal advance is a different proposition. We will examine the obverse side of this issue, concerning whether middle class images of society are distinctly hostile to collectivism, in a later chapter. For the meantime the focus is upon the working class where the issue concerns whether a preference for collectivism and a disinclination to seek individual mobility underlies manual parents' attitudes towards education.

There is an alternative explanation on offer as to why parental attitudes should be related to social class. Rather than composed of discrete segments, this explanation regards the class structure as a continuous ladder and spells out the implications for parental attitudes of standing upon different rungs. Similar 'success values' are attributed to all strata but it is argued that, in contrast to those already located near the summit, from a situation nearer the bottom, an equivalent desire for success will result in lower absolute levels of aspiration and less interest in climbing to the very top. In relative terms, to rise from unskilled to skilled manual status or from the latter to a lower level white-collar job represents as great an achievement as for the son of a bank clerk to become a doctor. According to this school of thought, the class structure may be segmented in terms of images of society and associated political affiliations but, in terms of mobility ideologies, there are no comparable breaks. Both manual and white-collar strata are regarded as finding the prospect of upward mobility attractive, but in absolute terms manual workers' aspirations, both for themselves and their children, are scaled down as a result of their modest starting points.

This 'implications of occupying different positions' line of thought is preferred by Raymond Boudon, the French sociologist and incorporated into his mathematical model explaining how inequalities of educational opportunity are generated.[18] The main current of support, however, has come from America where educational aspects of the issue have been set within a broader argument concerning whether or not it is valid to regard a modern society as functionally integrated beneath a set of consensual values. A number of investigators, including Empey[19] and Turner,[20] have examined levels of student aspiration and claim to have shown that, relative to their own positions, working class ambitions are, if anything, higher than middle class aspirations. It has also been found that when students are questioned about their 'fantasy' hopes for the future, the absolute gap between working and middle class aspirations closes substantially.[21] On the basis of this evidence Wan Sang Han[22] has argued that common success values pervade all strata in American society and that the modest absolute levels of working class aspiration that might initially appear to deny this can be explained partly with the relativity argument and, partly, as realistic adjustments to the exceptional obstacles that confront the working class striver. Caro and Philblad[23] have endorsed this latter argument, showing that lower class students' relatively modest aspirations result more from their perceptions of the difficulties that would be involved in moving to higher levels than from any working class evaluations of job opportunities according to different criteria than those employed amongst the middle classes.

Whether these arguments can be transposed to the situation in Britain will only be decided as the relevant evidence is made available, though one study conducted in the nineteen-fifties suggested close parallels.[24] However, there is evidence showing that, irrespective of parental and pupil values, individuals from working class backgrounds face exceptional obstacles en route to success and this evidence renders the 'implications of occupying different positions' argument at least circumstantially plausible. To begin with, the working class child's family, relatives and friends may be simply incapable of supplying advice and information on how to work the educational system. Parents who do not understand 'new' school subjects, who are unaware as to whether higher education is likely to eventually pay off in job opportunities and who, in the absence of any experience of student grants, worry over whether they will be able to afford to send a child to university, are obviously ill-placed to supply the push and encouragement that could help their children survive to the final stages of the educational competition. To aggravate this situation there is the culture-shock or strangeness often felt by working class pupils venturing into an educational world beyond their parents' and probably most of their friends' personal experience. Given these facts of working class educational life, it becomes easy to understand why parents and pupils should be willing to focus their ambitions on better-known and less distant terrain, particularly if an obstacle such as an only modest performance at O-levels is encountered on the way forward.

When account is taken of the limitations of their own experience and knowledge, it also becomes easier to understand why so many working class parents should feel that education is best left to the schools, and that parents should avoid 'interfering'. We do not need to postulate any antipathy towards the principle of getting on to explain either working class parents' apparent uninterest in education when set against middle class standards, or their readiness to subdue 'fantasy' aspirations. The relative absence of 'push' from the working class child's home need not imply that little value is placed upon personal achievement. The known facts can be alternatively explained simply in terms of the implications that follow starting from a working class position.

This diagnosis of the sources of inequality of opportunity leads to different proposed remedies than those associated with the mobility ideologies school of thought. The latter point of view has fuelled proposals for educational change aimed at making the culture of the school more consistent with working class values; developing community curricula with teaching materials related to working class life and removing the current emphasis upon competition and individual achievement. In contrast, the implications of occupying different positions theory has in some places, including Boudon's mathematically articulated model, led to a pessimism about inequalities of opportunity ever being redressed by educational reform.[25] If inequalities of opportunity are the necessary implications of children setting off from different starting points, then are they not likely to survive all forms of tinkering with education? According to this view, greater equality of opportunity cannot be used to generate but will only follow a movement towards more general social and economic equality enabling children to start their educational careers from more equal positions.

Other commentators, however, have interpreted the same evidence more optimistically and insisted that education can make a worthwhile difference. If the working and middle classes subscribe to basically similar success values with the former merely encountering the more severe obstacles, then could not the schools take an effective initiative in stimulating and harnessing the aspirations of working class parents and students? This type of thinking lay behind the Plowden Committee's proposals for positive discrimination. But is this thinking based upon secure foundations? Our study of class imagery enables this problem to be systematically examined. What are the deeper values and processes that underlie social class differences in attitude towards education?

Images of class and mobility orientations: the evidence

The previous chapter has explained how the mobility ideologies to which our sample subscribed were associated with their responses to a broader 'affective' cluster of questions which also encompassed feelings towards members of superordinate and subordinate strata and views regarding whether class differences were desirable and inevitable. We have seen that along this affective dimension as a whole, variations in manual respondents' answers bore no clear relationship to whether their images of society were middle class, proletarian or of another working class variety. We can now report that throughout the entire sample including both blue and white- collar workers, the types of middle and working class images that respondents exhibited displayed no consistent connections either with their answers to the 'affective' items *en bloc* or to the questions tapping mobility orientations in particular. Respondents who identified with a working class were just as likely as our self-assigned middle classes to both desire and expect to rise up the social scale into a higher class during their lifetimes (12 per cent and 10 per cent). A positive evaluation of upward mobility was neither confined to nor even concentrated within the middle classes.

All respondents were questioned about their personal career aspirations. They were asked whether they would like promotion to a higher level of work and the proportions of white and blue collar respondents giving affirmative answers (62 per cent and 55 per cent) were not dissimilar. A desire for personal mobility is by no means uncommon amongst manual workers, whilst it is incorrect to assume that white-collar employees are uniformly anxious to climb further up career ladders.

For the purpose of further analysis we 'pooled' three questions tapping affective orientations towards the class structure upon which the sample's answers were fairly evenly balanced and thereby distinguished a 'high scoring' group that answered 'positively', that is, in ways associated with desiring and expecting personal upward mobility, to at least two of these items. 'Working class' respondents (36 per cent) were actually more likely than 'middle class' informants (24 per cent) to fall into this high scoring group. In the area where our investigation was conducted the assumption that the manual strata would prove relatively devoid of ambition proved quite contrary to the facts.

According to our evidence it is entirely possible for a precisely developed working class awareness together with all that this is conventionally taken to imply including support for trade unions, the Labour Party and other measures intended to better the collective position of the working class, to co-exist alongside individual ambition. Why should individualist and collectivist outlooks be regarded as incompatible? There are many examples of individuals rising to personal fame and fortune as a result of their dedication to working class movements and our evidence suggests that these cases involve no exceptional duplicity. Rather than mutually exclusive, individualist and collectivist approaches are better regarded as different strategies to which the same persons can willingly resort depending upon their likely effectiveness in given situations.

Amongst the entire sample, positive affect in general and seeking personal mobility in particular were most evident at intermediate levels in the social hierarchy which cut across the white and blue-

Table 4:1

Mobility orientations, occupation and education

Respondents giving two or more 'positive'
responses to the three 'pooled questions'

a) % *in Registrar General's social classes:*

I	6
II	28
III NM	35
III M	33
IV	29
V	19

b) % *with post-secondary education:*

Full-time university course	4
Full-time course at a College of Education, CAT or Polytechnic	24
Full-time vocational course at a Technical College or equivalent institution	39
Part-time vocational course at a Technical College or equivalent institution	39
None	24

c) % *whose highest qualification obtained:*

Degree/professional	10
Semi-professional	23
Technical	44
School Certificate/GCE	34
None	28

Note: NM = Non-manual
      M   = Manual

Percentage replies relate to those respondents who answered relevant questions.

collar cleavage (see Table 4 : 1). In terms of occupational status, positive affect was at its maximum amongst skilled manual and lower level white-collar workers. Furthermore, whilst ambitious respondents did not differ from others in terms of inter-generational mobility experiences, they were distinguished by their experiences of intra-generational mobility via education. In terms of their educational histories, the highest scorers were those who had proceeded to an intermediate level such as a vocational course at a technical college rather than either those who had been through university or some other form of higher education on the one hand or those who had obtained no post-secondary education on the other. Similarly in terms of qualifications those with Ordinary National Certificates or something comparable outscored those with degree level or professional qualifications and respondents who had achieved nothing beyond secondary school exams.

Explanations must be tentative, but a desire for upward mobility and its associated orientation seems to become prominent amongst individuals who have fought through education's risky 'alternative route' and whose immediate career situations tempt a quest for further advance by offering at least the prospect of further mobility. Circumstances where individuals have established themselves above the base of the social hierarchy but not in touch with, though maybe in sight of its more prestigious layers, where there is the possibility, though not the certainty, of further career advance and where the adoption of higher strata as reference groups is, therefore, encouraged, appear liable to heighten individual ambition. Research conducted amongst high school students in America has suggested that aspirations tend to be pulled upwards in equivalent marginal situations. When students have some contact with higher strata such as through a mother who 'married down', or friends with high strata origins or ambitions to proceed to college, the aspirations of the individuals concerned are likely to be pulled upwards[26] and circumstances of this type can occur amongst both blue and white-collar workers and amongst persons who align themselves with either the working or the middle class.

In addition to their personal ambitions, respondents were questioned about their educational and occupational aspirations for actual or hypothetical children and, despite the unreality of the latter type of questioning, the overall pattern of response did not differ from where the aspirations related to real offspring. The results were exactly in line with the findings of American investigations in which a similar analysis has been attempted. In absolute terms, manual parental aspirations were modest compared with white-collar respondents' (Table 4 : 2, items a and b). However, in relative terms, when levels of parental aspiration were measured against respondents' own starting points, the relationship between occupational status and ambition disappeared (Table 4 : 2, items c and d). Whether thinking of themselves or their children, according to our evidence, there is no clear qualitative contrast between working and middle class mobility orientations.

In addition to direct questions about their levels of aspiration, we attempted to establish the extent to which the sample defined education as an important means of becoming mobile, for we recognised that although they might appear keen when directly questioned on the subject, manual parents in particular might not ordinarily regard schooling as a route to success. Accordingly, at separate points during each interview, respondents were asked how a father could best help a son, then a daughter, to get on in life and later a more

Table 4:2
Occupational status and parental aspirations

	Registrar General's social classes					
	1 n = 39	2 n = 121	3NM n = 83	3M n = 145	4 n = 63	5 n = 23
a) % who would wish a son to remain at secondary school until age eighteen or later	92	68	70	60	49	27
b) % who would wish a son to obtain a job in R/G classes 1 or 2	92	79	73	53	34	25
c) % who would wish a son to remain at school beyond their own leaving age	96	81	88	88	76	82
d) % who would wish a son to obtain a job above their own occupational level	—	40	47	40	79	50
e) % mentioning 'education' in response to each of three relevant questions	41	28	31	34	43	30

general question was phrased querying the qualities that determine 'who gets on'. Spontaneous references to education in answering these open-ended questions were coded to see whether manual respondents would prove as aware as the white-collar sample of the role that education can play in precipitating mobility. Once again, however, there was little difference between the regard in which education was held between these two sections of the sample (Table 4:2, item e).

Overall our findings unambiguously endorse the 'implications of occupying different positions' explanation of social class differences in attitudes towards education and are inconsistent with predictions from the 'contrasting mobility ideologies' theory, though whether this justifies the inference that common success values pervade all strata is debatable. Virtually every respondent recognised the possibility of a person moving into a different social class during his lifetime and it was certainly the case that at all levels in the social hierarchy the majority wanted their children to climb higher than themselves. But in terms of personal ambition the absence of any desire to rise into a higher class or job amongst many white-collar respondents may be considered as significant as its extent within the manual sample. A more valid conclusion would be that, given the particularly favourable histories and immediate circumstances described above, both white and blue-collar workers who identify with either a middle or working class will define upward mobility as desirable and seek to achieve it.

Not only does the 'implications of occupying different positions' argument best explain our findings, it is also particularly able to account for other known features of the relationship between attitudes towards education and social class. In terms of levels of parental ambition it is not the case that the population can be conveniently dichotomised into a middle class displaying uniformly high aspirations and a working class lacking any comparable interest. Absolute levels of parental aspiration gradually decline as the social hierarchy is descended and introducing the concepts of 'middle' and 'working class' is really an unnecessary intrusion. Convention may justify employing these terms as shorthand phrases to refer to the higher and lower levels of the social hierarchy but they only mislead if taken to imply the type of qualitative break that is found in class images, party political loyalties, trade union affiliations and related attitudes. There are no specifically working or middle class attitudes towards education in particular, or social mobility in general. To endorse this point, the views of our blue and white-collar respondents on the comprehensive education issue proved virtually identical. Slightly over a half of both groups expressed a preference for a comprehensive secondary system against one in which children were allocated to different types of schools on the basis of their assessed abilities. Since 1964 the movement towards comprehensive reorganisation has been associated with the Labour Party and, amongst its supporters, the comprehensive principle has been linked with the furtherance of working class interests. This is one instance amongst several where, as we shall see in later chapters, alignments in the party political system do not coincide with divisions of grassroots opinion between the major parties' supporters.

The fact that parental educational aspirations have been rising over time throughout the entire population is another piece of evidence that falls into place once the 'implications of occupying different positions' viewpoint is accepted. As the number of years of schooling obtained in their own childhoods by the adult population has increased, aspirations for the next generation of both white and blue-collar children have been pushed further upwards. Patterns of both historical change and contemporary variation in ambitions, whether parental or personal, are best explained as reflecting processes of adjustment to different immediate circumstances rather than the work of qualitatively distinct mobility ideologies.

Prospects for equal opportunity

What then are the prospects for equality of opportunity? Our evidence offers little encouragement to advocates of a non-competitive working class community school. Contrary to some previous suggestions, manual parents are no less receptive than middle class parents to the desirability of individual success and its pursuit through education. Working class parents are as likely as middle class parents to see education as means of 'getting on' and to value it for this reason. A working class community school that ignored the 'rat race' and worked alongside the local community in preparing its children to participate in that community's own way of life would engender no greater enthusiasm than the secondary modern.

Our evidence suggests that existing working class mobility orientations are a foundation upon which an achievement-oriented school system can build. Attempts to stimulate parental interest and boost levels of aspiration, if conceived imaginatively seem likely to elicit a favourable response. Positive discrimination, if expediently pursued, is likely to pay off. But there is other evidence from our enquiry suggesting that the chances of any considerable movement towards equality of opportunity are bleak. As others have inferred upon facing the 'implications of occupying different positions', educational change is probably less potent than we might prefer to hope as a means of redistributing life-chances.

Education is often discussed in terms of how it can facilitate upward mobility. We more rarely note that education can also be a route down the social scale. When commentators do draw attention to how children fail, this invariably prefaces a call for the doorways to success to be unlocked. Although researchers have diligently enquired as to why more working class children do not climb higher up the educational and social ladders, it is rare for investigators to consciously explore why the schools do not downgrade more middle class children. Of course, upward mobility is a more palatable subject than downward mobility. It creates a better image for education to treat it as an avenue to success rather than as a route to failure. Campaigning for the schools to downgrade more middle class children would hardly be a popular platform. Nevertheless, there can be no ignoring the fact that upward and downward mobility are complementary processes. Changes in the shape of occupational structure such as the relative expansion in white-collar employment, and also an influx of immigrants, can make it possible for upward mobility amongst the native population to exceed downward movements, but pulling more working class children into higher strata than structural and demographic trends necessitate must require that more middle class children be pushed down. And it can clarify the relationship between social class and educational achievement if the conventional presentation of the problem is inverted, attention focused upon downward mobility and consideration given as to why more middle class children are not allowed to slide down the hierarchy.

In our investigation we collected information about both objective and subjective aspects of respondents' past mobility experiences. We asked about their fathers' occupations and were able to identify patterns of inter-generational mobility and also invited respondents to estimate subjectively their own class positions in relation to their fathers'. The information obtained suggested that, amongst our sample, downward mobility was usually unacknowledged and psychologically quite unacceptable. Comparing respondents' occupations with their fathers' in terms of the Registrar General's classes, 31 per cent were defined as immobile, 50 per cent as having moved up and 19 per cent as having slid down. In terms of respondents' own assessments of their histories, however, a different picture appeared; 65 per cent believed they were in the same classes as their fathers, 24 per cent felt that they had been upwardly mobile and only 4 per cent defined themselves as having descended. The class divisions that respondents recognised were clearly not identical with the Registrar General's, and complete symmetry would have been most surprising. Overall, respondents recognised fewer class divisions and were therefore less likely to regard themselves as mobile than the Registrar General's more discriminating scale indicated. However, respondents who in objective terms had moved up the hierarchy were more likely to acknowledge subjectively their mobility than those with objective histories of descent. Only 4 per cent defined their class positions as lying beneath their fathers', so had we relied solely upon the sample's subjective estimates, we would have unavoidably concluded that downward mobility was virtually non-existent in the area where the enquiry was conducted.

A series of questions, probing the issue from different angles, indicated that downward mobility was held in negative regard by our respondents. When questioned about parental aspirations, virtually no one named an occupational or educational level lower than his own. When asked whether each subject would prefer to be in a different class than the one where he had already said he belonged, approximately a third indicated that they would rather have been in higher groups but absolutely no one expressed a preference for membership of a lower class. When questioned about their attitudes towards persons in the classes beneath their own, approximately a quarter of our respondents stated that they 'admired' such individuals but 4 per cent only 'wished they were like' them.

In so far as our results are typical, downward mobility is a prospect that holds little attraction in our society and, in this respect, there is every reason to believe that our findings are representative of a wider public. There has been some debate as to whether social mobility itself leads to inter-personal and psychological maladjustment. There is evidence suggesting that upward mobility can be institutionalised, anticipated and cushioned so as to minimise potential strains.[27] With downward mobility, however, the evidence unequivocally points to a relationship with mental illness and previous enquiries, like our own, have portrayed downward 'skidders' as anxious to avoid recognising their descent and insisting upon retaining attitudes characteristic of their origins.[28]

Failure to admit and recognise downward mobility usually involves no strenuous self-deception. With life-styles and standards of living changing over time, inter-generational comparisons are not straightforward. Furthermore, the boundaries between classes recognised amongst the public are blurred as we found when questioning respondents about the determinations of individuals' class positions. Income, wealth, power, education, life-style, occupation and attitudes were all mentioned with many interviewees naming more than one characteristic. Hence it requires no exceptional gymnastics for the manual son of a white-collar father to extend the boundaries of the middle class downwards to include himself and his peers. Class boundaries are flexible and, when necessary, income and life-style rather than occupation may be emphasised as the key factors. Downward mobility is unattractive but individuals can normally avoid acknowledging that it has happened to them without undue difficulty.

These prevalent attitudes towards downward mobility invite

suspicion that, as far as education is concerned, parents with privileges to conserve will do whatever is necessary to ensure that their children do not slip. If educational innovations succeeded in boosting levels of working class aspiration and attainment, it is entirely likely that, given the scope, middle class parents would raise their sights and encouragement to still higher levels. From a position near the top of the class structure, the dangers of demotion are inevitably more threatening than when viewed from other levels. With considerable inequality of opportunity persisting, it might appear that heirs to privilege should feel secure but this misunderstands their predicament. In a social hierarchy in which there are many more positions around the bottom and centre than at the top, the chances against any person becoming mobile into the élite will necessarily be immense; say, only one in twenty. However, to continue with this hypothetical but realistic figuring, for those who start at the top, even when protected by considerable inequality of opportunity, if the élite numbers only 10 per cent of the total population there will be a greater than one-in-two chance of any individual suffering downward mobility. 'The implications of occupying different positions' perspective illuminates the behaviour of the privileged as well as the underdogs.

When examining the social class-educational attainment relationship we certainly need to pay attention to the lower strata and ask amongst other things, why in absolute terms their levels of aspiration and interest are modest. However, if the conduct of middle class parents who refuse to allow their children to slide is also considered problematic the overall situation can be clarified. If society-at-large genuinely deems greater equality of opportunity to be desirable, it will be necessary to think in terms of either compressing general socio-economic inequalities or somehow restricting the opportunities available for children from privileged backgrounds to stay ahead and if these suggestions are politically inexpedient, the prospects for significantly greater equality of opportunity remain bleak.

Education and social control

In acting as a channel through which social mobility can occur, education has been regarded as performing two functions for the wider social system. First, education has been seen as contributing to society's efficiency by allocating talent to positions where it can be exploited to the advantage of the community-at-large. Hence the concern surrounding the 'wastage of talent' in the working class pool of ability. Second, education has been seen as performing a social control function, not so much through the overt teaching of approved values as through the hidden curriculum of the selection process, its effectiveness as an apparatus of control depending upon the appearance of opportunities for ascent being greater than the reality.

The prospect of mobility through education can be regarded as syphoning discontent amongst society's less privileged away from challenges to the structure and distribution of privilege itself and into the pursuit of personal advance within the social system as it exists. By appearing to provide opportunities for all, education can be regarded as a safety-valve for society-at-large but, since the economy needs more men on its assembly lines than company directors and, therefore, the highest levels of success can be reached by only a few, the educational route to the good life can be trod by only a minority. So for the educational competition to perform a social control function its appearance must conceal a less benign reality. With the majority who cannot be successful education must persuade them that they have been offered a fair chance and that their subsequent exclusion from privilege is not an injustice inflicted by an unfair society but simply reflects their own lack of talent.

In a number of discussions of how class inequalities are maintained without provoking crippling dissent, writers have attached considerable importance to this educational safety-valve[29] and there is ample evidence that, in the recent past, education in Britain has indeed operated to such an effect. If it did not establish equality of opportunity, the 1944 Education Act together with its resultant eleven-plus and secondary moderns seems to have convinced the majority of working class children that they were being given a fair chance and denied success only because they were personally ill-equipped to share in power and privilege.

However, whether the educational syphon is still effective and, even more so, whether it will continue to be a safety-valve in the future, are debatable matters. Rather than placating the population, our enquiry's evidence invites suspicion that education may increasingly become a source of disaffection. To begin with, our data suggest that individualism and collectivism do not stand in an either/or relationship. Individuals can seek personal advance without support for collectivist measures to improve the conditions of the strata to which they currently belong being undermined. Education may syphon off and channel individual ambition but it will not anaesthetise collective grievances.

Second and equally important, as Earl Hopper has pointed out,[30] for a modern education system to perform a social control function it requires a delicate balance to be struck between 'warming up' and 'cooling out' students' aspirations and in Britain this balance may have been achieved only during a passing historical phase. In the first place, everyone has to be warmed up, motivated to join in the competition for success through education before some can eventually be convinced that they lack the necessary ability. Before 1944, when access to secondary and higher education was impossible for children from many working class families, it is unlikely that this all-round warming up occurred and had our survey been conducted in that era, it is doubtful whether the majority of working class parents would have displayed ambitions for their children to realise through education. In this period, disclaiming all hope of mobility through education would have been a realistic adjustment to the situation of the British working class and hopes for individual betterment in all probability would have been channelled elsewhere.

Since 1944 all children have at least entered a national educational competition and consequently aspirations have been warmed up. In other words, as evidenced in the results of our enquiry, individual ambition has been substantially syphoned into education. For the social control function to operate, however, a subsequent cooling out process must also occur, which defeat in the eleven-plus, followed by daily reminders of one's limitations in the lower streams of a secondary modern, seemed to achieve in an admirable manner. But just as there is nothing inevitable and historically permanent about warming up, so with the cooling out part of the equation. Unless the latter process is effective, the safety-valve can turn into a source of discontent by escalating aspirations to levels that cannot be satisfied and this may well be the current trend in British education.

Both the eleven-plus and the practice of streaming within schools are in decline. The trends are away from early selection and towards delaying failure until even later stages in the educational process. Opportunities for all children to obtain qualifications in comprehensive secondary schools are widening, while beyond secondary school the trends are towards growing proportions of young people who will embark upon careers throughout all levels in the white-collar sector, and skilled manual workers as well, obtaining at least a taste of the opportunities that further and higher education can offer. The data from our enquiry suggest that future generations who move upwards through the educational system in this manner will do so with full parental support. At all levels in the social hierarchy, parents want their children to use education to climb to higher positions than they themselves have achieved and the educational system itself is responding to these aspirations.

What seems unlikely is that the opportunities to which education can lead will grow correspondingly. Rather than functioning as an apparatus of social control which it probably did with increasing efficiency between the nineteenth century and the nineteen-fifties, education's selection process may be on the way to acting as an additional and growing source of disaffection in the social system. If in the contemporary historical situation working class mobility orientations are not hostile to either personal advance in general or mobility through education in particular, therefore, this may not be the commonly supposed sign of a safety-valve in action. The actual implications may prove completely different.

5. A Class for Itself?

Class awareness and class consciousness

In discussing class images and mobility orientations, we have referred to different forms of class awareness but deliberately avoided that more provocative term, class consciousness. In the interests of both clarity and convention, the expression 'class consciousness' is best reserved for the special case where individuals are not only aware of belonging to a particular class, but recognise the interests that all members of their class share and how these conflict with the interests of other classes, leading to support for economic and/or political action to further their own class interests. Given such a strict definition, in Britain the fully class conscious worker must be considered exceptional. But to what extent does a growth of working class consciousness remain a possibility?

In the nineteenth century Marx predicted that in capitalist societies a polarisation would juxtapose the bourgeoisie and proletariat and this prediction has haunted subsequent discussions of the working class. To be fair, it must be pointed out that Marx never anticipated the working class becoming united into a revolutionary force overnight and, throughout his works, was concerned to clarify the impediments. In the long run, however, Marx believed that the experience of factory conditions, collective urban life, impoverished standards of living and the constant threat of unemployment would gradually make members of the proletariat conscious of their common and exploited situation. As a result Marx argued that the class in itself would become a class for itself and trade union activity together with participation in reformist political movements were seen as interim stages in the making of a revolutionary proletariat.

Obviously enough, this has not yet happened. Capitalism is still with us and the workers are not yet manning the barricades. Manual workers in Britain are not even solid in their support for the Labour Party let alone a revolutionary socialist movement. But there have always been latter-day prophets prepared to argue that the apparent stability of capitalist societies is fragile and that the polarisation rather than the embourgeoisement of the working class is imminent.[1] Since the mid-nineteen-sixties it has been possible to refer to a left-ward shift in the Labour Party and trade union leaderships and a rise in working-time lost due to strikes as signs of imminent polarisa-tion and, although comparable pointers have been appearing since Marx's lifetime without the awaited revolution ever ensuing, these arguments cannot be dismissed out of hand. After all, it is the case that in objective terms the gap between the propertied rich and the working population remains as wide as ever, and at least a prole-tarian class awareness is present amongst sections of the manual labour force. Given a crisis situation, therefore, it is not out of the question that the working class could be transformed into a revolu-tionary body and in the Britain of the nineteen-seventies such a crisis situation may be not too far away, for it is widely accepted amongst economists, though less widely broadcast by politicians, that the balance of trade coupled with the situation created as a result of de-clining domestic profit-margins since the fifties requires real wage levels to be depressed in order for the economic system to survive.[2] Given the necessary depressing action, it may not prove correct but it is by no means ludicrous to argue that working class loyalties could solidify and a revolutionary situation result.

Westergaard and Resler are amongst those who insist that the mass radicalisation of the working class remains a distinct possibility. To these writers, the main lines of class division in contemporary Britain are clear and simple. They insist that the range and shape of income inequality in Britain reflect the fact that the economy is still, in all essentials, 'capitalist',[3] while 'Property, profit and market — the key institutions of a capitalist society—retain their central place in social arrangements and remain the prime determinants of inequality'.[4] According to Westergaard and Resler, analyses such as presented in the previous chapters of this book can only obscure the basic clea-vage in the class structure. 'It has become standard practice, in the formally agnostic conventions of academic sociology, to underline the complexity of patterns of inequality in contemporary western societies. The practice is misleading. There is complexity of detail. But to focus on intricacies in this corner and that is to obscure the simplicity of the picture as a whole.'[5] These writers are content to interpret the entire history of government economic involvement and the growth of the welfare state during the twentieth century as 'the evolution of an alliance between business and state agencies, with organised labour encouraged to accept a place as a third partner provided that it agrees to the essential pre-conditions of the alliance: the maintenance of private property and profit as the mainsprings of the economy'.[6] In discussing the state of the working class, Westergaard and Resler insist that its orientations are 'quasi-Marxist'. They dismiss portraits of the working class as particularistic, hedonistic and devoid of any future perspective—characterisations that have found no support in the pages of this book. While acknowledging that radical orientations are interspersed with pragmatic acceptance and accommodation, Westergaard and Resler stress the significance of long-standing working class commitments to a broad labour movement harbouring visions of a better society and are alert to developments that could strengthen these elements in working class awareness including the exposure of the cash nexus as the sole tie between labour and capital, the decline of particularistic local communities which can limit the horizons and ambitions of their members, the rise of shop-floor militancy and escalating wage expectations that capitalism cannot contain. How plausible is this revolutionary scenario?

The class struggle

It is perhaps too easy to dismiss talk of the class struggle and class war and to convince oneself that these ideas have no relevance in this day and age. We know that workers are no longer on the breadline but have colour televisions, that trade unions offer protection against arbitrary management—some would say that they run the country—that everyone has the vote and has been accorded a range of civic rights extending from education to retirement pensions. Talk in these terms and the class struggle can seem very far away.

Yet in point of fact there is a class struggle every day in every factory. Maybe it is rarely consciously thought of as a class struggle but it is exactly that. Managements are constantly trying to increase production, to keep down wage costs and to use labour in what appears to managements to be the most efficient manner which, depending on the situation, may mean introducing a shift system, measured day-work, speeding-up of the production line or urging flexible transfers of manpower from job to job. None of this means that managers are malicious or oppressive as individuals. They may be congenial characters and recognised as such on the shop-floor but the system forces managements into a class struggle. Firms have to be profitable and this requirement works its way through so that, at department levels, supervisors are judged by results.

Needless to say, the workers on the receiving end play their parts in this struggle and this is not because they are malevolent trouble-makers but simply because they are forced into opposition by the system. Workers must constantly try to prevent the pace of work becoming too oppressive and struggle to ensure that real earnings are edged up rather than down. As with managements, exactly what this means must depend upon the situation. It may involve fooling the work-study man, bargaining over bonuses and piece-rates or get-ting control over the speed of the assembly line. Far from the class war being dead, all these are daily issues throughout industry.

This is not to say that strikes, go-slows, overtime bans, sabotage and other forms of overt unrest are daily events in most factories. As some trade union leaders like to remind us, over 99 per cent of all working time is not lost in industrial disputes. The point is that there is a class struggle under way even when people are working 'normally'. As already admitted, the situation may not ordinarily be seen in these terms. In their own eyes, most managements are simply trying to run their factories in the most efficient manner. For their part, most workers are probably intent upon protecting no one apart from themselves, their families and, possibly, their immediate mates. Nevertheless, from a wider perspective it is possible to discern a pattern of conflict recurring right across the industrial system and to call it a class struggle is no flight of fancy but just realism.

If all workers saw the situation in these terms the working class would be class conscious and the long-awaited revolutionary situa-tion would have arrived, but just as it may be obvious that a class struggle is in process it is equally clear that the fully class conscious worker remains the exception. In his study of Ruhr steelworkers, Popitz[7] found that although nearly everyone subscribed to a form of us/them imagery, only one per cent were genuinely class conscious in the Marxian sense and full-blooded class consciousness was simi-larly rare amongst the respondents in our investigation.

Workers cannot be unaware of conflict in their work situations, but while recognising that they share collective interests with others, the others are often only the rest of the work-group, department or factory rather than the entire working class. Similarly, while the exist-ence of an opposite side will be recognised, this may only be the par-ticular employer involved or even the site management. There is no automatic transition from these glimmerings of class awareness to seeing one's own situation as but one small part of a societal class struggle. Hence the struggle remains mostly localised and the work-

ing class remains far from fully class conscious. In Marxist terminology, the working class is generally limited to a trade union, factory
or contingent consciousness.[8]

Ideological hegemony

What prevents the escalation of factory consciousness into working
class consciousness? Amongst contemporary sociologists the most
popular explanation is ideological hegemony.[9] According to this
account, workers are locked into exploitive class relationships not
by the more naked forms of military and political coercion that were
prominent in the past but by dominant conservative ideas. This ideological hegemony theory contains two complementary arguments.
The first suggests that values legitimising the status quo emanate
from privileged strata, filter downwards through education, the mass
media, churches and political parties—and produce acquiescent instead of revolutionary responses amongst the less privileged. The
claim that the ruling ideas in any age are the ideas of the ruling class
is no mere tautology but follows the observation that those with economic and political power enjoy privileged access to the means of
communication.

Acquiescence can be promoted by encouraging individuals to
interpret their predicaments in other than class terms by, for
example, propagating a national identity with the privileged strata
portrayed as the leaders. Alternatively, acquiescence can result from
suggestions that the current distribution of privilege is fair and just,
that the wealthy are only reaping their entitlement and that in-
centives are essential to the prosperity of the entire community. Additionally acquiescence may be fostered by suggesting that the solutions to life's problems lie not in a re-casting of class relationships
but in the afterlife, or washing machines, beer, football and other
leisure pursuits. It hardly requires systematic research to establish
that the main channels of mass communication in Britain are more
committed to conveying such values than stimulating working class
solidarity. For sceptics, however, the chapter and verse is available
for consultation.[10]

The second and complementary argument in the ideological hegemony theory points to the failure of potentially radical organisations
in Britain, principally the trade unions and the Labour Party, to
propagate a genuinely revolutionary ideology. To grasp this argument, a point to be understood is that human beings do not respond
to stimuli in the deterministic way that is true of the subject-matter

in the natural sciences. People are able to think, to acquire and manipulate ideas, and how they react to any circumstances, therefore, will depend not only upon the objective character of these circumstances but more directly upon the interpretations that are placed upon them. Given the basic facts of the contemporary worker's situation, including an income below the national average and being constantly on the receiving end of authority, it is not inevitable that the subjects will join trade unions, strike, become committed revolutionaries or anything else. There is a variable quality to the response. Given its situation, the working class will always be susceptible to trade unionism and related appeals but the messages need to be sold. This is why ideas can be hegemonic. It is also why the working class needs converting to trade unionism, socialism and certainly to class consciousness and, hence, the importance of intellectuals, parties and working class movements that can espouse revolutionary ideologies.

Competent observers are agreed that in Britain the Labour Party and trade unions have never propagated revolutionary aims but there is some debate as to why these organisations should have traditionally taken a moderate and reformist line. On the one hand, there is a conspiracy or manipulationist viewpoint which argues that the electoral system, education and other apparently liberal and democratic institutions were deliberately introduced and initially structured in ways that have kept them permanently responsive to the interests of privileged classes. The franchise, for example, was extended to the working class in stages with the respectable sections in the forefront, thereby allowing a 'responsible' working class political movement to emerge before manhood suffrage was introduced.[11] Similarly the first trade unions to be recognised were 'responsible' bodies representing the aristocracy of labour.[12] Likewise in education, opportunities in the secondary schools were opened to working class children in stages which enabled the state to consolidate the traditional role of these schools in educating an élite. The proletariat may never have become class conscious but, at times, the more privileged strata in Britain seem to have possessed sufficient understanding of their vital interests to act as a ruling class.

Other commentators have explained the moderation of the British labour movement by stressing some version of Robert Michels' iron law of oligarchy.[13] This iron law suggests that in becoming organised, as is necessary to marshal the mass support required to act as a revolutionary force, even socialist movements that are initially dedicated to democratic ideals create oligarchic and conservative tendencies within themselves. The very fact of organisation creates a division between leaders and led, the formers' life-styles come to resemble that of more privileged strata, their organisations become integrated into the existing social system, encumbered by tactical compromises, and functionaries gradually become more committed to the 'means' they have instituted than their movements' original ends. This theory offers an account as to why leaders and their organisations should often appear to betray the working class rank and file and, in Frank Parkin's view,[14] helps to explain why the social democratic parties that have enjoyed periods in office in western countries have executed moderate 'meritocratic' rather than 'egalitarian' policies genuinely designed to redistribute privilege in favour of the working class.

These twin explanations of the docility of western labour movements can be considered complementary. Internal 'revisionist' tendencies are no doubt strengthened by a receptive external environment and there can be little argument about the end result; that working class organisations in Britain have never been powerful advocates of revolutionary ideas. Hence hegemonic values emanating from the dominant strata have encountered little resistance.

Talk about hegemonic values might sound plausible but how does one prove the case? In so far as manual workers subscribe to conservative values, can we conclude that they have been imposed from above? We can research the content of mass communication but it is more difficult to directly study the genesis and impact of ideas. The obvious rejoinder to the hegemony viewpoint is to argue that revolutionary sentiments have taken little hold simply because manual workers correctly realise that moderation is in their own best interests. Testing the hegemonic values theory is partly a matter of putting the historical evidence together piece by piece. In addition, however, it is supported by survey evidence from enquiries like our own. There is greater agreement throughout the white-collar than amongst the manual strata upon values endorsing acquiescence in existing social arrangements such as opposing extensions of public ownership and feeling that trade unions ought to co-operate with employers to enlarge the common cake rather than bargain to increase their members' proportion (see Table 5:1). Blue-collar workers support such values to a degree but only alongside contrary oppositional values that are less strongly evident elsewhere. Whilst falling short of proof, this evidence is consistent with the view that acquiescent values filter down the social scale with consequences that can be termed an ideological hegemony.

One example of these hegemonic processes in our investigation concerned the sample's perceptions of pay differentials. We asked respondents to name the groups they considered had done best and worst in terms of pay increases during recent years and, although contrary to the objective evidence in 1972, nearly every white-collar interviewee named a manual group as having made the greatest gains. Dockers, car-workers and miners were frequently mentioned. Although contrary to the evidence in the sample itself, the belief that the middle classes were being overtaken was prevalent. Most manual respondents endorsed this view of their own strata faring relatively well, though within the working class there was greater dissent from this dominant opinion and considerable belief that some groups of manual workers were amongst those who had done worst (see Table 5:2), but the crucial point is that (as Table 5:3 shows) amongst manual

Table 5:1

White- and blue-collar attitudes towards public ownership and trade unions

	White-collar n = 243	Blue-collar n = 231
	%	%
Views on more public ownership		
In favour	24	37
Against	76	63
Agree that 'trade unions have too much power'	66	45
Preferred trade union tactics		
a) Increase workers' share	14	25
b) Co-operate with employers to produce bigger shares for both	86	75

respondents the belief that their strata had been advantaged in terms of recent pay settlements was related to expressed satisfaction with their own earnings. This is just one example of hegemonic values' ability to nurture acquiescence.

Exponents of the ideological hegemony theory are broadly agreed on the end result. They agree that conservative values such as the belief that trade unions should co-operate with employers are not totally absorbed because they conflict with manual workers' everyday experience. The end product, according to Michael Mann, is that most manual workers remain confused by the clash between conservatism and proletarianism, but touched by both.[15] Parkin sees the situation as one in which dominant values are negotiated to fit the realities of working class life so producing accommodative responses, meaning that inequalities and deprivations may be accepted, but fatalistically rather than enthusiastically.[16] Perhaps,

Table 5:2

Occupational status and some perceptions of income distribution

	1 n = 39	2 n = 119	3NM n = 82	3M n = 141	4 n = 62	5 n = 23
	Registrar General's social class					
	%	%	%	%	%	%
Belief that white/blue-collar income gap has:						
widened	5	23	23	19	36	38
narrowed	90	71	67	66	40	29
other	5	6	10	15	24	33
Manual group named as having done best in recent pay increases	89	91	89	87	84	91
Manual group named as having done worst in recent pay increases	24	38	30	57	58	83

however, this is too smooth a verdict, and maybe Mann's emphasis on the inconsistency and confusion that riddle manual workers' attitudes is more authentic.[17] Mann points out that consensus across all strata is most pronounced at the level of very general and abstract values such as support for Parliament and the Queen. At the level of concrete experience norms, however, this consensus begins to break down and proletarian opposition amongst the manual strata comes into evidence. Many manual workers remain unconvinced as a result of their own first-hand experience that, for example, the interests of employers and employees are in harmony. The lofty values

Table 5:3

Perceptions of income changes and views on own pay (blue-collar workers)

	Blue-collar workers who believe that the gap between white- and blue-collar income has—	
	narrowed n = 125	widened n = 57
	%	%
Views on own pay		
Very well paid	22	11
Adequately paid	44	40
Underpaid	30	42
Other	4	7

where consensus reigns may be too abstract to guide day-to-day behaviour but despite this, Mann insists, they have important consequences. Their effect is to prevent any coherent, alternative and
radical ideology along with a vision of an alternative society developing amongst manual workers, with the result that working class
opposition is spasmodic, ill-co-ordinated and localised.

Amongst hegemonic dominion theorists there is some debate concerning the prospects of a revolutionary working class consciousness
breaking through. Mann and Parkin both believe that such a development will require very emphatic encouragement from above in
the form of a socialist movement, initially supported by intellectuals
and maybe a small vanguard of the proletariat strenuously propagating a revolutionary ideology. Moorhouse and Chamberlain,[18] in
contrast, inspired by a sample of rent strikers' doubts as to the 'rights
of property' and disaffection with established political processes,
have challenged this pessimism. All agree, however, that the basic
requirement before a revolutionary situation will occur is that the
working class must break from the ideological hegemony which currently results in false or inauthentic forms of consciousness.

Impediments and alternatives to class consciousness

Are hegemonic values the only crucial obstacles and would a
genuinely revolutionary consciousness be the only authentic response to the predicament of the working class? Is a class conscious
proletariat awaiting the opportunity to appear given the necessary
crisis situation coupled with the requisite ideological leadership? In
our view this diagnosis over-simplifies a more complex situation and
there are other obstacles that make the polarisation of the British
working class into a revolutionary force a most remote possibility.

To begin with, although there may be a daily class struggle in industry this is rarely more than but one ingredient in the situation.
There are other equally authentic elements in the worker's social
reality that compete for attention. As previous research has demonstrated, our own enquiry found that in different ways and to
admittedly different degrees, nearly all respondents were positively
attached to their jobs. Most employees like their work and are not
eagerly awaiting a revolution that will rid their lives of this institution. It is misleading to think of the man on the assembly line as
the typical manual worker. Only approximately 2 per cent of the
labour force is engaged upon mechanised line or belt work. For those

who are, the experience can be anything but pleasant; it can be boring and monotonous as the cheers testify when the track breaks down in car assembly plants. But there are skilled workers in particular whose jobs are intrinsically rewarding, while others find that the people they work with make doing the job pleasant. In addition to this, workers are not only workers but also have homes, families and leisure. They need not treat work as a central life interest but can develop an instrumental approach in which their expectations, as far as intrinsic job satisfactions are concerned, are modest and easily satisfied.

The idea of abolishing work even in a fantasy situation such as a pools win holds slight popularity. Furthermore, there is little more boring than being on strike, going slow or working to rule. Aside from any financial damage involved, for others, apart from the few activists who can be at the centre of affairs, waging the class struggle can be intensely depressing.[19] So attitudes towards work are generally mixed. Work may be an arena of conflict but, at the same time, it can be a source of various satisfactions and individuals can psychologically disengage instead of pressing for change in response to whatever irritations are encountered.

Another impediment to class consciousness concerns the manner in which the working class is splintered by numerous cross-cutting internal divisions. Some are hierarchical, as between different levels of skill, while others are lateral as between different but equally skilled trades. From the sidelines these divisions can appear trivial when set against the common interests that all workers share but from the hub of the working class they look anything but petty. Particular crafts possess their own traditions and loyalties that have been harboured over generations and initiation may require a prolonged apprenticeship. The resultant occupational communities may foster a sense of 'us' and 'them', but the 'us' within which individuals are emotively bound need not encompass the whole of the working class. Indeed, rather than promoting it, intense craft loyalties can inhibit the growth of any wider class solidarity as, according to Brown and his co-investigators, has been the case amongst Tyneside shipbuilders.[20]

Many employees are as concerned with differentials in status and earnings vis-à-vis other groups of workers as with pursuing a common struggle against employers. Hence the intractable problem of low-paid occupations. In principle everyone is in favour of helping the low-paid but, at the same time, other groups want to maintain their relative standing, so the low-paid continue on relatively low pay. Concern over differentials and relativities are as much part and parcel of shop-floor life and occupy as central a place in the history of trade unionism as the class struggle, and they cannot reasonably be dismissed as false consciousness. The factory, firm and trade are real entities with which ordinary workers can identify and ideas about a wider class struggle often cannot compete.

Yet a further obstacle to the development of working class consciousness is the absence of a clearly defined other side. The existence of a well-defined enemy can always help bolster solidarity amongst an in-group but, for the working class, the 'them' in the us/them equation are not easily identified. The working class is not a caste and its boundaries are blurred. There is no single factor that decides whether or not a person belongs to the working class and this indecision is fully reflected in public opinion. Furthermore, as explained in the previous chapter, members of the working class often possess individual ambitions for themselves and their children. Many have relatives who have already 'got on'. So, against which opposition would a class conscious proletariat side?

It is easy for theorists to name capitalists, bourgeoisie or property owners, but these are just names rather than social formations that workers encounter in their daily lives. In any case, there remains a huge cushioning middle ground between these proffered enemies and the strata who identify themselves as working class and it is with this soggy centre, largely occupied by bureaucratic officialdom, that the day-to-day class struggle is usually fought. It is also this middle ground into which many workers would like themselves or their children to rise. Individuals can be ambitious for themselves without weakening any desire to improve the conditions of their current strata and proletarian workers are as keen to get on as other sections of the population. This illustrates how far away even proletarian workers remain from genuine class consciousness. Attitudes towards superordinate strata are too mixed for the class struggle to become a whole-hearted occupation.

By definition, the working class is class aware but, nevertheless, the class conscious worker is the exception. Workers are involved in a class struggle and perceive this aspect of their circumstances with varying degrees of clarity but rarely with total commitment. Notions of a class struggle and appeals to class loyalties strike a chord amongst most groups of working men, but it is only one chord amongst many that are being regularly triggered. This is why working class organisations such as trade unions have a constant struggle to maintain interest, enthusiasm and solidarity and, to the extent that solidarity is intermittently achieved, its boundaries rarely cover the entire working class.

What this amounts to is that the failure of a revolutionary proletariat to surface cannot be entirely attributed to ideological oppression. This is only one part of the story for a more basic truth is that
the class struggle is just one aspect of the manual worker's everyday
reality. Class consciousness is one possible response but it is not the
only authentic reaction. There are several features of the worker's
situation that encourage other responses and this is why the polarisation of the working class into a revolutionary force may remain a
possibility but is very unlikely.

The future of the working class

The cleavage dividing the blue-collar strata from the rest can be made
to appear deep or shallow depending upon the type of evidence introduced. The most marked disparities between the blue and white-
collar strata were itemised in chapter two. They cover subjective class
identities, party political loyalties and trade union membership.
Focus upon this information and the hiatus separating the blue from
the white-collar strata appears considerable. However, we are not
entitled to overlook that in our own and other comparable investigations, on questions tapping individuals' views on specific issues such
as public ownership and trade union power, most blue-collar
workers endorsed the majority white-collar position.

In one sense, the whole of the above discussion has been an attempt
to define the significance for modern society of there being a self-
aware working class that tends to vote Labour and to organise itself
in trade unions, so there should be little doubt that we consider
this cleavage to be of continuing importance. But this does not
justify playing tricks with survey data and forgetting the contrary
evidence.

On specific socio-political issues dissent from the generally dominant point of view is certainly stronger amongst manual than non-
manual workers. Taking individuals' attitudes on specific issues
alone, however, although one would rightly conclude that the
manual strata are a base for the development of oppositional values,
it would be difficult to argue that the class structure is marked by
a major cleavage dividing blue-collar workers from the rest. At the
level of specific issues, many common values are found throughout
the population with the working class being merely a section where
dissent is relatively common but still the exception to the rule. This
may be partly attributable to an ideological hegemony maintained
by superordinate strata, but explaining the facts does not explain

them away. In reality the working class character of the manual strata is compartmentalised and sufficiently divorced from attitudes on specific issues to stultify its impact as an oppositional force.

The evidence implying a severe cleavage between the blue and white-collar strata can be alternatively interpreted as suggesting that this particular division in society is recognised and effectively accommodated within the social system possibly even to the extent of being over-institutionalised. Oppositional values distinguishing the blue-collar strata may have ground more deeply during the historical period when alignments in politics and industry that persist to the present were originally taking shape. Today, however, much of the institutionalised opposition of the working class, apparent in its membership of trade unions and support for the Labour Party, resembles a hollow shell. Trade union membership was the norm amongst our manual respondents but it was only exceptionally accompanied by an ideological commitment to a working class movement. The most common reason for joining a trade union, given by 49 per cent of our blue-collar members, was the operation of a closed shop. Similarly, the majority of our manual respondents voted Labour and sometimes explicitly accounted for their party loyalties in class terms. The Labour Party retains considerable electoral support because it is identified as a working class party and, for this reason, to hold its 'traditional' vote the Party needs to maintain a distinctly working class appeal. At the same time, however, when it comes to propagating and executing a programme of socialist reform including a frontal attack upon existing structures of economic power and privilege, such as by extending public ownership, the enthusiasm of Labour's working class supporters can quickly evaporate, creating a dilemma of which the Party's leadership is well aware. The blue/white-collar schism is real and has been institutionalised to play a central role in political and industrial life, but it is a division that fails to penetrate grass-root attitudes in a thoroughly convincing manner.

Faced with this evidence it might seem obvious to infer that change must be imminent. Is there not a strain towards consistency built into the human psyche? Must we anticipate that before long manual workers will either abandon their 'nominal' working class identities, trade union and Labour Party loyalties or else become a more solidly radical force?

Each of these prophecies has earned some support from analysts who have perused the seemingly contrary evidence just presented. However, it may be too easy for people who make an occupation out of intellectual pursuits to exaggerate the importance of intellectual coherence in social life at large. Others are not punished or rewarded to the same extent as sociologists depending upon whether the things they do, think and say are consistent. It is entirely possible for individuals to live comfortably with contradictory attitudes that are brought out and put away depending upon the prompts. People are not ordinarily under the pressure even to make them conscious of the inconsistencies in their outlooks, let alone to mould their beliefs into coherent wholes.

The working class, therefore, constantly puzzles investigators who find it difficult to make sense of their contradictory findings. In Brown's study of Tyneside shipbuilding workers, for example, the views expressed during interviews proved anything but militant but this did not prevent militant industrial action occurring during the period of the investigation.[21] Depending upon the immediate situation, men will down tools and talk a militant language or feel favourably disposed towards their jobs and employers. One wonders which evidence gives the true picture and the answer is that both pictures are true. Different situations strike different chords and there are no pressures demanding overall coherence. It is mistaken to assume, therefore, that pressures are at work which, given time, will iron out inconsistencies in working class attitudes and behaviour.

Researchers normally like their findings to fall into tidy patterns. Failure to discover statistical or otherwise meaningful relationships between variables is often considered an indictment of the research itself. Hence there is always a temptation to forget the evidence that does not fit. Michael Mann is one of the few investigators willing to face the inconsistencies in the results of his own research, and once the ambiguity is tolerated, then as Mann illustrates, many acute insights concerning the state of the working class become available. Following fieldwork amongst manual employees in Peterborough, Mann concluded that 'neither the workers as a whole, nor any identifiable sub-group possessed a coherent belief system'. Mann proceeded to observe that, together with those sharing in societal power, 'only those who seek to change society need to encompass it intellectually'.[22] Ideological consistency is a luxury that the working class can manage without and, in order to understand the working class, this is a fact that must be squarely faced. As Mann argues, 'There is no need for working class people to develop beliefs that legitimate or illegitimate society so long as they recognise the *factual* need to comply with its demands',[23] meaning that individuals are quite capable of working for capitalist concerns without being ideologically committed to capitalism as a socio-economic system—and similarly workers can vote Labour and join trade unions if their interests seem to be served by doing so without being committed socialists or subscribing to any other coherent, radical ideology.

The intention is not to portray working class people as irrational, muddled and incapable of logical thought. Manual workers are as able to think coherently as anyone else. As we have shown, when blue-collar workers are appropriately questioned they are perfectly able to present coherent images of society and to give entirely rational accounts of their careers, hopes for their children and political loyalties. The argument is not that the working class is peculiarly incapable of intellectual coherence but that manual workers are rarely constrained to see society as a whole, decide upon the structural alterations they would prefer, and align their behaviour and more specific beliefs accordingly. There is nothing akin to the sociology seminar amongst popular working class pastimes.

Although there may be only one working class, therefore, and even if its ideological tendency is proletarian, it does not follow and, indeed, there are pressures described above contending otherwise, that it must eventually become a class for itself. Perceptions of conflict in the work situation are only occasionally totalised and linked to a vision of an alternative society, and there is more than the awaited crisis combined with effective ideological leadership inhibiting such developments. On balance, therefore, it seems most unlikely that the working class will evolve into a revolutionary force liable to re-shape society.

As argued in an earlier chapter, the historical trends are narrowing even that degree of proletarian solidarity and associated ideological precision that sections of the working class have achieved but this does not mean that the manual strata are going to become docile and acquiescent. Progressive embourgeoisement is as unlikely as polarisation. There are no grounds for suspecting a movement towards a conservative coherence. A slackening of proletarian solidarity need not mean a decline in working class dissent. What we are more likely to find is working class dissent becoming increasingly fragmented and expressed outside the institutional framework that the Labour Party and trade unions have provided. Paradoxical though it may seem, any decline in working class solidarity must necessarily undermine established procedures through which dissent has hitherto been channelled. So strikes are not withering away as was forecast in the nineteen-fifties but industrial disputes are now mostly unofficial and it is difficult for trade union leaders to guarantee any social contract on behalf of their members.

Given the continuing blue-collar predicament, being paid visibly and considerably less than managers and professional people, the flat career pattern and limited access to housing and related life-chances outside the work situation, there is going to remain a working class that can never be organised into total acquiescence. For society at large, therefore, the working class remains an unstable and continuing challenge but not a revolutionary threat.

6. The Modern Organisation and the New Middle Class

In discussing the middle class an initial danger is assuming that we are considering simply an opposing side of a coin. On the other hand we have a working class relatively disadvantaged in terms of income, career opportunities and access to housing—circumstances that co-alesce to produce an oppositional working class culture in which manual workers are immersed to various extents. White-collar workers are relatively advantaged and in this sense clearly comprise the opposite side. It is easy to imagine, therefore, that their privileged circumstances must generate a counterpart and conservative middle class culture. But is this actually the case?

In his research Webb[1] found that middle class Conservative voters were less likely than working class Labour voters to explain their party loyalties in class terms. The Conservative Party attracts little support by being regarded as a middle class party. There could be various reasons for this, but such evidence must at least arouse suspicions that although most white-collar workers describe themselves as middle class just as blue-collar employees identify with a working class, being middle class might not imply quite the same feelings of loyalty and awareness of common interests that arise amongst manual workers.

There is considerably more inequality amongst non-manual than amongst blue-collar workers. In terms of income levels, for example, the white-collar range extends from the clerk in the town hall to the managing director, whereas blue-collar earnings are relatively tightly compressed. Similarly in education, most blue-collar workers left school at the earliest opportunity, while amongst the white-collar strata there is a more even distribution from 'early leavers' to those with post-graduate qualifications. Collectively non-manual workers are relatively privileged vis-à-vis blue-collar employees, but there is considerable inequality amongst the privileged. Regarding everyone above the working class as an undifferentiated 'them' might seem plausible from within the working class, but the majority of white-collar employees can hardly be expected to place themselves in the same ranks as the rich and powerful.

The social sciences have always been problem-oriented. The tendency has been to study people who possess or are felt to pose problems. Hence the numerous studies of working class communities and the more depressed the more likely they are to have commanded sociologists' attention. Prosperous suburbia, in contrast, remains relatively virgin territory and therefore we know less than we might about the middle classes.

Obviously enough, the middle classes are an important part of the community. Numerically they include around 40 per cent of the population and must therefore affect the character of life in our society. Apart from their numerical weight, however, it is also the case that the middle classes play a key role in most types of organisations. The middle classes supply the leaders and activists even in organisations such as the Labour Party with predominantly working class memberships, while community groups ranging from parent–teacher associations to photographic societies are mainly middle class bodies. It does not imply any ideological bias to argue that the middle class makes society tick. There are good and obvious reasons, therefore, for wanting to know exactly what goes on inside the middle class. And rather than prejudging the issue at this stage, whether the middle class is a similar type of entity to the working class is better left an open question.

The waning middle class

Shortly after the Second World War, when British society was apparently being re-cast by its first majority Labour government, Roy Lewis and Angus Maude produced a study of *The English Middle Classes*.[2] A quarter of a century later their arguments inevitably appear dated, but the book is still worth reading because it engenders an awareness of the changes that have occurred during the intervening years.

Lewis and Maude believed that there was a middle class culture incorporating a set of distinctly middle class values. They argued that a number of factors played a part in defining the middle class. To be middle class was to practise a particular type of occupation — white-collar, to enjoy a particular level of income — above average, to have received a particular type of education — at grammar school and/or university, and to live in a good, comfortable house in a good, respectable area. Lewis and Maude argued that these circumstances crystallised to produce a middle class style of life and set of values. Their middle class culture was based upon possessing at least modest amounts of wealth together with reasonable incomes, which furnished a sense of independence and a desire to conserve assets. Equally importantly, in Lewis and Maude's view, these circumstances allowed the middle classes to develop tastes and interests in 'high' culture and gave them the platform required to supply initiative, leadership and ideas in political and economic life.

Lewis and Maude made no secret of their admiration of the middle class. They regarded the middle class as the backbone of the country. It was middle class savings, enterprise and other qualities that had given Britain its greatness. What is more, Lewis and Maude were worried by what they saw as a decline of the middle class. They argued that the middle class was being squeezed economically by the 1945 Labour government along with powerful trade unions, and also psychologically, by the propagation of working class and radical ideologies which seemed to be leaving the middle class feeling guilty and over-privileged. Lewis and Maude, therefore, believed that middle class life-styles and attitudes were under attack and were concerned about this, not only because they sympathised with the middle class and its life-style but also because they believed that the prosperity and quality of life in the country as a whole depended upon the survival of middle class values.

Other books appearing at that time were driving home essentially similar arguments. For example, in his study of the *Middle Class Vote*[3] John Bonham argued that as a minority group in an age of democracy, the middle class would inevitably find its interests neglected by the major political parties. Bonham portrayed the middle class as standing hopelessly compressed between big business on the one hand, which was able to look after itself, and the working class with its trade unions on the other, and finding little protection in a democratic political system.

These sentiments have lived on. Surveys still find many white-collar workers who feel that they are being overtaken. Professional people still sit in detached houses surrounded by spacious gardens and talk about the erosion of their standards and how the rug of merited privilege is being pulled from under their feet. In the early nineteen-sixties, Runciman found that the majority amongst a national sample of white-collar respondents believed that, in terms of levels of income, most manual workers had become better off,[4] and a more recent study of technicians has assembled similar complaints about salaries being overtaken by wage levels.[5] Magazine articles still talk about the plight of the waning middle class, and in 1975 an ITV programme was devoted to 'The Mangling of the Middle Classes'. However, we are no longer being entertained to serious books like Bonham's, and this is because in objective terms the middle class has clearly not declined to a point of extinction. Whatever some laymen might still believe, objectively any narrowing of differentials over the last fifty years has been no more than marginal. Blue-collar incomes, on average, still lag behind white-collar salary levels. Properly informed analysts, therefore, no longer write about the waning middle class.

Indeed, contrary to immediate post-war fears, far from declining, the middle class has grown in size as the development of the economy has created new white-collar jobs in the professions, administration, management, science and technology. Since the nineteen-fifties it has been more common to hear claims that we are becoming a middle class society. But in the process of growing the middle class has become a different type of social formation than the middle class with which Lewis and Maude sympathised. Lewis and Maude's archetypal representatives of the middle class were self-employed businessmen and independent professional people such as doctors and solicitors. They were men of substance and independence who represented an ideal that other persons, maybe doing only routine office jobs but with pretensions to middle class status, could admire and emulate. No one who has examined the middle class during the last twenty years has used these as representative figures. There has been general agreement that the middle class is changing. But in what direction? And is it any longer possible to identify a core middle class culture comprising a coherent set of values and an associated style of life?

Organisation and corporation men

The organisation man thesis, which takes its title from a book produced by W. H. Whyte in 1956,[6] is one of the better-known attempts to chart the course of change within the middle class. Whyte's theme was the replacement of the small enterprise by the large-scale organisation and, related to this, the demise of the self-employed man and the rise of the salaried manager. This trend has undoubtedly been occurring. It has happened in industry and also in education so that, for example, the universities today are rarely informal places where at least all the staff recognise each other. Nowadays everyone works for 'it'—the organisation. Whyte's fame arose not because he simply drew attention to this trend, but on account of the implications he claimed to have identified. The growth of the large-scale organisation, according to Whyte, was related to a shift in attitudes and life-styles. Whyte believed that the protestant ethic was being replaced by a social ethic. The protestant ethic is the outlook of the rugged, entrepreneurial individual who values personal initiative and success. The social ethic, in contrast, is purportedly nurtured in organisations where life is governed by rules and established procedures that generate an emphasis on fitting in and handling people. The valued character in such a setting is not the abrasive, get-up-and-go type, but the chap who nestles in, learns to belong, works co-operatively with the group and who does not disturb established procedures.

In *The Organisation Man* Whyte was not dispassionately describing a trend, but expressing deeply felt reservations about the direction in which the society in which he lived was heading. Whyte's dislike of the organisation man was no secret. He argued that creative, imaginative persons stood to be penalised under the social ethic and, therefore, that firms and indeed society as a whole were liable to lose their dynamic thrust. In addition Whyte argued that the social ethic required individuals to sell their personalities to their organisations, in the process of which happiness was liable to be sacrificed. Part of Whyte's argument was that the demands of the organisation led to a shallow, superficial life outside the workplace. Whyte painted a distinctly unattractive picture of middle class suburban life. His organisation man was a transient character moving from house to house and suburb to suburb as the organisation moved him from job to job. In Whyte's view, organisation man's prime loyalty had to be to his employing organisation and, therefore, in his neighbourhood he was able to sink only shallow roots. He might participate hyperactively—joining clubs and visiting neighbours—but, accordingly to Whyte this is mostly superficial for next year or next month organisation men realise that they might have to be enjoying doing different things with different people.

Whyte's was just one amongst several books to draw attention to the significance of the large-scale organisation. The same theme, the rise of the corporation man at the expense of the older entrepreneur, was at the fore in C. Wright Mills's *White Collar*.[7] According to Wright Mills, across all levels of white-collar employment—professional, managerial, sales and clerical—personnel are being drawn into corporations. Also, as with Whyte's polemic, rather than an exercise in value-free social science, Wright Mills's work was intended as a critical appraisal of contemporary trends. Wright Mills had little affection for his corporation men. He argued that in addition to selling their labour, white-collar employees were also required to sell their 'selves' to the corporation. Managers and salesmen, for example, are expected to appear to believe in what they are doing, whereas the blue-collar worker at least is not required to fit his personality to his job.

Where Wright Mills took his argument beyond Whyte's was in pointing to the political significance of these trends. Wright Mills believed that whatever their numerical weight, the new white-collar strata were socially and politically impotent. Wright Mills's corporation man was capable only of 'making out', that is, seeking happiness and comfort within the circumstances that his work and income permitted. Having sold himself to the corporation, he was limited to seeking personal solutions to what Wright Mills believed were often public problems. Hence an ethos of political indifference; a willingness to accept social and economic predicaments as beyond challenge. Wright Mills believed that, for the present at least, the white-collar strata were incapable of combining into a cohesive class with a definite political ideology. They were restricted to carving out reasonably satisfying lives for themselves and their families within circumstances that simply had to be accepted.

Other well-read books of the fifties developed broadly parallel arguments. For example, David Riesman and the co-authors of *The Lonely Crowd* [8] talked about the demise of the inner-directed man, the individualist who is urged on by inner values that he cannot betray, and the rise of the other-directed man whose main concern is to adjust and fit in. Like Wright Mills, Riesman was alert to the political implications of this trend. The era of the other-directed man, he forecast, would be an age of what has subsequently been termed 'consensus politics' in which the business of political activity involves adjusting and reconciling different interests rather than fighting ideological battles in defence of firmly held values.

In his essay on 'Bureaucratic Structure and Personality', Robert Merton also took up the theme of the effects of large-scale organisations upon their members. [9] Merton's argument was that the experience of working in a bureaucracy amidst detailed rules and regulations tended to produce a rigid personality, concerned with following correct procedures and resistant to change. This is not *exactly* what Riesman, Wright Mills and Whyte were saying. Indeed, each of these authors had something distinctive and original to argue. But there was a common thread running through their work that began with the fact of large-scale organisation, proceeded to identify its implications for the employee's personality, and then drew out the broader social, economic and political implications of the spread of the personality type in question.

An additional theme running through this literature was the tone of social criticism. None of his early biographers portrayed the organisation man in glowing terms. Indeed, if books such as Whyte's and Wright Mills's were used for careers guidance purposes it is doubtful whether there would be many aspirants for work in large corporations. Rather than its architects and beneficiaries, these works portrayed the new middle classes as victims of social change.

Whatever their other merits, the creators of the organisation man thesis were persuasive. The works discussed above were all American but their theme has been taken up throughout the western world. As far afield as Japan equivalent arguments have appeared about the 'salary man' who is tied to his organisation by the security offered but only in exchange for total loyalty.[10] The influence of the organisation man thesis has not only been a result of the wide readerships that its authors gained. More importantly, the central ideas have been circulated second-hand through magazines, newspapers and broadcasting and to some extent it was the resultant popularised image of middle class life that provoked a new type of radical dissent during the nineteen-sixties. We were told, via pop culture, that our little houses on the hillsides were made of ticky-tacky and that the careers about which we were so concerned were really not worth having. Young people, especially students on American campuses, appeared to find this message convincing, for the protest movements in which they became involved did not resemble the more familiar revolts of the oppressed. The new radicals rejected even what counted as success, the comfortable middle class life-styles, offered by the society in which they lived, a rejection that Charles Reich subsequently heralded as 'the greening of America'.[11]

Persuasively written sociology can be influential, but this is never sufficient proof of its validity. It was easier to write sociology in the grand style, surveying the past and envisaging the future, when there was only scanty evidence from research to take into account. Since the classical statements of the organisation man thesis appeared, however, research has begun to accumulate into the life-styles and values of the middle class. So the question we now have to answer concerns exactly how well the thesis stands up in the light of the evidence now available. Is this rather pessimistic portrait of the new middle class really valid? We intend to show from the evidence of our own and other relevant investigations, that however many chords it still strikes the thesis must be subjected to several modifications and, when these have been made, little of the original argument remains standing.

The traditional and compressed middle class

The first qualification is that not all white-collar workers are organisation men, nor are they likely to become so. Whyte and Wright Mills probably exaggerated in order to make their points as forcibly as possible, which is a legitimate tactic, but in appraising their arguments a more balanced perspective is desirable. To begin with, the evidence now available shows that it is entirely possible for individuals to hold white-collar jobs in organisations without becoming organisation or corporation men in the senses that Whyte and Wright Mills used these terms.

In research conducted in organisations it has become common to distinguish pure bureaucrats from professional employees such as doctors and accountants whose qualifications and membership of professional associations can decrease their dependence upon their immediate employers. The professional man can use his professional body as a reference group and source of norms to guide his work — and consequently, it is possible for such individuals to be employed in large organisations while remaining something more than mere cogs in a machine. It is also the case that some white-collar workers join trade unions and the large organisation has proved the unions' most fertile recruiting ground, implying that the corporate environment does not always leave individuals as placid and impotent as suggested in the classic statements of the organisation man thesis.

The places of highly qualified professional people and trade unionists within the middle classes will be discussed in more detail in subsequent chapters. The very existence of such groups, however, at least narrows down the scope of the organisation man thesis, and also endorses the doubts expressed earlier, about whether it is still useful to imagine any single type as representative of the entire middle class.

Apart from the new men—the white-collar trade unionist and the salaried professional employee—it is also important to remember that more traditional middle class characters are far from extinct. The proportion of self-employed persons in Britain has been declining—from 6·7 per cent of the working population in 1911 to 3·4 per cent in 1966, but there are still thousands running small workshops and retail businesses. However untypical he is becoming, capitalist economic systems still allow a role for the small-scale entrepreneur.

Bechhofer's research amongst shopkeepers in Edinburgh suggests that it is their love of the independence that keeps many in self-employment.[12] Whilst their incomes were not usually less than they could have hoped to gain from employment, the hours of work of the retailers were long and, therefore, earnings expressed as an hourly rate were often modest. But maintaining a valued independence made the effort worthwhile. A comparable picture of the persistent and reliant self-employed emerged in our own study, though many were considerably more prosperous than Bechhofer's retailers. There were 39 self-employed persons amongst the 243 white-collar workers that we interviewed and, as can be seen from Table 6:1, they were amongst the most prosperous members of our entire middle class sample. Some were in no sense affluent but, on average, the incomes

Table 6:1

The economic status of white-collar employees and self-employed workers

	Employees n = 204	*Self-employed* n = 39
% working 51 hours per week or more	14	46
% whose 'leisure' occasions are used in non-leisure activities	11	19
% with annual earning of over £3500	9	40
% car owners	81	95
% who own more than one car	16	41
% who possess telephone	76	97
% who own stocks, shares, etc.	24	61

of the self-employed were unusually high, even by white-collar standards and their life-styles were well flushed with the fruits of prosperity such as second cars. The self-employed were often genuinely wealthy, enjoying not only high incomes but possessing investments, in their own businesses of course and frequently on the stock market as well. At the same time, as in Bechhofer's study, our self-employed respondents could not be likened to the idle rich. They worked exceptionally long hours—nearly a half worked for over fifty hours in a typical week—and when questioned about their uses of a number of evening and weekend 'leisure' occasions they proved almost twice as likely as white-collar employees to be engaged in non-leisure activities.

This type of entrepreneurial middle class can be found in all parts of Britain. In his study of middle class families in Swansea, Colin Bell[13] was able to distinguish the family and neighbourhood life-styles of 'spiralists' who worked for organisations and moved around the country as their careers unfolded, from 'burghers', the locally born trades and professional people who were mostly running family businesses and practices. Most towns contain a comparable local bourgeoisie and however much the national economy might become dominated by the large-scale enterprise, individuals working on their own accounts are unlikely to be completely superseded. Self-employment can still be very rewarding, not only because of the independence it offers but also, in many cases, in respect of its economic returns.

Where the self-employed scored relatively badly compared with other groups of white-collar workers in our sample, was in terms of education and qualifications. As evident in Table 6:2, they were less likely to have attended grammar, direct-grant or independent

Table 6:2

White-collar education and employment status

	Employees n = 204	*Self-employed* n = 39
% who left school aged 14/15	42	50
% who attended grammar, direct grant or independent school	49	41
% with no post-secondary education	28	53
% with no professional or similar qualification	38	58

schools and lacked the higher education and professional qualifications that have become common amongst men pursuing organisational careers.

Politically our self-employed respondents stood slightly to the 'right' of the white-collar strata as a whole (see Table 6:3). As we shall see below, there is evidence that along with other more traditional sections of the middle class, the self-employed feel that their positions are threatened and, therefore, that they could be susceptible to the appeal of ideologies promising to bolster their insecure privileges. The self-employed know only too well that small businesses are in decline. Thousands of new businesses are established each year but even more are ceasing to trade. The self-employed feel threatened not only by working class power, but also from places where they believe they ought to find support. Many feel exploited by larger and more powerful businesses that are slow to settle debts, under attack from local authorities with their escalating rate demands, and under continuous pressure from central government with its tax and national insurance impositions. During the first half of 1975 membership of the National Federation of the Self-Employed grew from 5000 to 40,000 before organisational disputes led to this movement's temporary collapse. The self-employed are still very much alive and are unlikely to die quietly.

The overwhelming majority of our self-employed respondents described themselves as middle class, but were less likely than other white-collar workers to regard this class as a broad stratum securely occupying the middle ground in the class structure. As we shall see in the next chapter, this was the type of middle class imagery most common amongst our sample. The self-employed, however, were amongst those who tended to define the middle class in deviant terms, one of these deviant definitions being to regard the middle class as a small group, compressed between a larger working or lower

Table 6:3

White-collar employment status and socio-political attitudes

	Employees n = 204	*Self-employed* n = 39
% who voted Conservative at previous general election	70	83
% in favour of further nationalisation	25	20
% who approve of Enoch Powell's views on immigration and race relations	60	51
% who believe trade unions have too much power	64	77
% in favour of comprehensive secondary schools	56	51

class and still richer and more powerful superordinate strata. This particular type of middle class imagery was prevalent amongst all sections of the traditional middle class, meaning not only the self-employed but other white-collar workers including managers and administrators who had risen to their positions in traditional ways, that is, as a result of long-standing service rather than on the basis of formal qualifications.

The title 'compressed middle class' is appropriate because, to begin with, this type of imagery defines the middle class as a narrow stratum squeezed between its neighbours. Furthermore, when asked which class they considered the most powerful, individuals who subscribed to compressed middle class imagery were exceptionally likely to name a subordinate group, usually the working class. This and other information about the compressed middle class is condensed in Table 6:4. These individuals felt insecure and exposed to threats from beneath while, at the same time, many were conscious of lacking allies amongst their economic equals and betters. Like the self-employed, other respondents who regarded themselves as belonging to a compressed middle class enjoyed higher incomes than were typical amongst the white-collar sample as a whole. They were men who had 'got on', but were less likely than others of equivalent occupational and economic status to have benefited from a higher education and to have acquired professional or equivalent qualifications. This was one source of their insecurity. Also, as evident in Table 6:4, these respondents were less likely than other white-collar workers

Table 6:4
Corollaries of compressed middle-class imagery

	'Compressed middle-class' n = 40	All white-collar respondents n = 243
% with annual income £3500 or over	26	15
% who believe the position of class they regard as most powerful is below own	30	13
% who received no post-secondary education	61	68
% completely satisfied with:		
a) jobs	40	50
b) promotion prospects	10	19
% who voted Conservative at last general election	72	72
% in favour of further nationalisation	38	24
% who believe that trade unions have too much power	63	66

to express complete satisfaction with their jobs and promotion prospects. They saw themselves as a disadvantaged group compared with the 'new men' by whom they were increasingly surrounded.

At first sight the political attitudes of our compressed middle class appear a strange mixture and certainly do not add up to a coherent ideology. They definitely felt no affinity with the working class. Conservative voting was as solid as in any other section of the white-collar sample and hostility to trade union power was equally pronounced. At the same time, however, there were hints of radicalism quite untypical of the middle class as a whole, illustrated, for example, in the 38 per cent favouring an extension of public ownership.

It is tempting to reach for convenient labels—incipient fascists,

Poujardists, petite bourgeoisie—but all these labels are too glossy to be meaningfully applied to an as yet incoherent social phenomenon. The fact is, however, that there are many individuals in positions that a generation ago would have entitled them to feel 'solid' members of the middle class but who now feel exposed and insecure. Internally they are a mixed group. They are threatened in different ways and from different directions. All they share in common is that the historical trends threaten their once secure middle class privileges. They are not radical by nature or habit, but feel unhappy with features of the world in which they live. They are aware of being in a minority that is being overtaken by new men and vaguely resent this. Consequently they can be attracted by certain radical values, but in Britain an ideology to crystallise these feelings and bind this section of the middle class into a social movement has yet to appear.

The old middle class is being compressed and while its heyday may have been in the nineteenth century our evidence suggests that it is far from moribund. A major effect of the growth of large-scale organisations concerns the manner in which they have altered the positions of middle class groups that they have not totally replaced but simply surrounded. Its traditional representatives are not disappearing but lingering on as a deviant and vaguely disaffected body within the new middle class.

Bureaucracy and personality

The second qualification to be attached to the organisation man thesis concerns whether the personalities of office-holders are really as moulded by their organisations as the classic statements suggested. Wright Mills wrote about, 'the small creature who is acted upon but does not act ... who never takes a stand ... pushed by forces beyond his control ... bored at work, restless at play'. This type of statement awakens archetypal impressions of the small-minded bureaucrat that have been sustained by generations of music hall comics. But to what extent are these impressions valid?

Melvin Kohn noted that 'observers of bureaucracy, impressed by its need to co-ordinate many people's activities, have assumed that a primary effect of bureaucratisation must be to suppress employees' individuality'[14] and conducted an enquiry amongst over 3000 males representative of the American adult population to test this view. He divided his sample into those who did and did not work in bureaucracies defined, for the purposes of the study, by features including size and the levels of authority they contained and addressed a series of questions to probe respondents' attitudes and social values. He aimed to discover whether working in a bureaucracy was really associated with any particular personality type. His results showed, however, that most of the correlations were small and secondly, that the relationships that did exist ran in exactly the opposite directions to those postulated in the organisation man thesis. Kohn's bureaucrats placed more rather than less value upon self-direction than other employees, they were the more open-minded, more receptive to change and less dogmatic in standards of morality. There was no evidence whatsoever of bureaucracies producing placid conformists. If anything, the reverse applied.

Table 6:5
Size of firm and political attitudes of white-collar workers

	Size of firm	
	Up to 100 employees n = 108	*501 and over* n = 73
% who voted at previous general election:		
Conservative	73	72
Labour	26	25
% in favour of further nationalisation	28	19
% who approve of Enoch Powell's views on immigration and race relations	58	57
% who believe trade unions have too much power	64	65

Our data also suggest that the organisations in which they work make less difference to employees' attitudes and values than critics of large-scale organisations have supposed. As Table 6 : 5 shows, apart from being somewhat less sympathetic to the idea of further nationalisation, the political attitudes of white-collar workers in 'bureaucracies' with over 500 employees differed little from those in small firms containing labour forces of less than 100. Views on issues such as divorce, abortion, contraception and the status of women are summarised in Table 6 : 6, and also display no clear relationship with organisational size. On the other hand, workers in bureaucracies did not appear to be even slightly more liberal or receptive to new values compared with other white-collar employees. As Kohn also recognises, our evidence suggests that more than a corporate environment is normally required to decisively favour the appearance of an open-minded liberalism. As we shall see, these qualities are associated closely with higher education and the possession of 'qualifications' rather than the immediate organisational contexts in which individuals work.

Kohn claims that rather than being oppressive, the large organisation can offer an especially liberating and enriching environment by providing higher pay, greater job security, and more complex and demanding tasks than the smaller firm. Instead of restricting the employee's personality, therefore, Kohn argues that large organisations can offer a secure base upon which he can consolidate his own values and develop a life-style reflecting his personal preferences. In Kohn's view 'man in bureaucracy' can remain far from bureaucratised. The classical organisation man theorists assumed that the rule-

Table 6:6

Size of firm and white-collar attitudes towards some social issues

	Size of firm	
	Up to 100 employees n = 108	501 and over n = 73
% who approve of married women working	36	40
% approving of equal pay for women	85	95
% approving of 'Women's Lib.'	41	36
% approving of free contraception on demand	69	62
% favouring liberalising the abortion law	19	22
% favouring making divorce easier	14	17

bound working lives of corporations' employees would turn them into habitually rule-following people. Kohn stands this argument on its head, focusing upon the complex tasks and security that large organisations can offer — and suggesting that bureaucracies are likely to turn their employees into especially independent persons. Our own findings suggest that this over-exaggerates the effects of the work environment, which leaves less of an imprint upon the employee than might be imagined. Large organisations do not leave their workers outstandingly independent and open-minded, but nevertheless, our results agree with Kohn's in showing that they certainly have no stunting effects of the type that Whyte and Wright Mills imagined.

Other writers have supported Kohn in suggesting that the real working life of the bureaucrat is less restricting and oppressive than first impressions might indicate. Crozier investigated 358 clerks in six Paris insurance companies,[15] and at an initial glance the jobs performed by these 'slaves of bureaucracy' appeared the epitome of boredom. But Crozier explains how the working lives of his clerks were much richer than first impressions suggested. He describes how, in a large organisation, everyone can move up a career ladder even if their movements take many individuals nowhere near the top and how, as this happens, individuals find their work becoming more interesting and involving. According to Crozier, the office worker is not turned into an unthinking slave. As his career progresses he acquires a sense of security and independence within the organisation. Consequently employees are able to develop their own private worlds and games that can involve 'beating the system', or helping or tricking each other, so making life at work anything but sheer, drab monotony.

Table 6:7
Size of firm and rewards from employment (white-collar respondents)

	Size of firm	
	Up to 100 employees n = 108	*501 and over* n = 73
% rating job security 'very good'	42	53
% who desire promotion at work	50	63
% with annual holidays of more than 22 days	49	63
% given 'sick pay' by employer	68	90
% working more than 51 hours per week	20	12
% with annual earnings of more than £2500	26	38

Lansbury's research amongst managers in a large organisation offers comparable evidence.[16] Like all other investigators who have actually interviewed bureaucrats about their jobs, Lansbury found that most were very positively involved in their work. Indeed for many, work was a central life interest, reflected in the number who said that they would continue in their jobs even if they 'won the pools' and work became financially unnecessary. Within his sample, Lansbury found various career orientations and also that different types of work were associated with different uses of leisure, but there was no group about which it was possible to talk of their organisational careers requiring independence and personal happiness to be sacrificed.

Our own findings wholly confirm this impression. Many advantages of employment in a large concern were evident, while the losses were far from obvious. As Table 6:7 shows, amongst our white-collar sample those working in large organisations enjoyed the longer holidays, the shorter hours of work, the better sick-pay benefits, were the more likely to rate their job security as 'very good', to desire promotion and to be enjoying above-average earnings.

Organisation men undoubtedly exist in the sense that there are people employed in large corporations. It is also the case that large organisations make demands upon their employees that are less likely to arise in smaller concerns. Whether this need involve employees sacrificing their 'selves' and happiness, however, is debatable. J. M. and R. E. Pahl conducted an investigation[17] amongst a group of managers whose circumstances, in many respects, seemed to illustrate all the ills associated with organisational careers against which Whyte and Wright Mills launched their tirades. The majority of the Pahls' managers had changed jobs at least once every five years and only a half were currently living within a hundred miles of their parents. Most of the managers had been pulled around the country in the service of their organisations and few had planned their careers in advance. The Pahls' managers were not self-directed, go-ahead types, shaping their own careers. Promotions had mostly been 'accidental'; a better job had been offered and taken and in so far as the managers had ambitions they were rarely striving to reach the top. A more typical aim was to reach a plateau on which to settle. Not only their work histories but also the social lives of the managers had to reflect their organisations' requirements. Few had any 'friends'. They all had 'acquaintances' including people they knew and liked at work, but the demands of their jobs coupled with the geographical mobility prevented day-to-day involvement in circles of friends outside the workplace. Wives and families also had to bow to organisational demands. Very few of the managers' wives were in paid employment. It was difficult for the wives to hold jobs when required to move home and district whenever their husbands' careers demanded. In addition the wives found their social lives constantly disrupted by the moves they had to make.

But to what extent was all this a sacrifice? The Pahls' research also shows a positive side to the manager's life and career. Most of the wives who were interviewed accepted their circumstances. They believed it was only right to put their husbands' careers first and many enjoyed the frequent moves to new and usually better areas and housing. Many also enjoyed the business of joining new clubs and making new friends in their shifting localities. The managers themselves were keen on their work and careers and in no sense appeared wretched or unhappy. They obtained many personal satisfactions from their working lives, felt involved in their jobs and derived a sense of achievement from their careers as they moved up and gradually acquired more money and influence within their organisations. There were few overt complaints about the 'rat race' from either the managers or their wives although, as the Pahls point out, the potential for disillusion was there.

Our investigation confirms that large organisations make distinctive demands upon their employees but, as already illustrated, they offer special rewards. The information summarised in Table 6:8 shows that respondents in large organisations had changed jobs

Table 6:8
Social corollaries of size of firm (white-collar respondents)

	Size of firm	
	Up to 100 employees n = 108	501 and over n = 73
% always lived in same area	29	19
% holding three or more different jobs during working life	41	51
% reporting three or more 'close friends' at work	14	25
% meeting three or more people from work socially	21	25
% reporting three or more 'close friends' amongst neighbours	41	54
% membership of clubs/associations	46	53
% use of recent 'leisure' occasions:		
non-leisure activities	12	10
television	32	28
entertainment	4	8
active	25	32
social	27	22

more frequently than those working for small concerns and were less likely to have spent the whole of their lives resident in the area where our enquiry was conducted. Job mobility rates amongst managers have doubled during the last thirty years,[18] and this no doubt reflects the growing prominence of large-scale organisations. Day-to-day patterns of leisure behaviour seem affected by this type of career; within our sample 'social' uses of leisure were less common amongst employees in large organisations than amongst other white-collar workers, while a greater proportion of free time was allocated to 'activities'—doing things rather than people. The careers of our organisation men required them to make friends wherever they could be found; hence there was more socialising amongst colleagues at work and neighbours and membership of clubs and associations was more common than amongst other white-collar respondents. The large organisation makes demands that affect its employees' non-working lives. In these effects, however, the gains and losses seem to balance one another.

There can be no argument, therefore, that the growth of the large-scale organisation has wrought changes amongst the middle class. It offers a special type of work environment and is associated with distinctive life-styles outside the workplace. At the same time, however, the evidence now available will not sustain the classic statements of the organisation man thesis. There is no evidence of large-scale organisations leaving an especially acquiescent imprint upon employees' socio-political values. Furthermore, the overall occupational and social rewards of a career in a large organisation appear at least to balance any sacrifices. While it is true that the middle class has been drawn into the large corporation, therefore, the real consequences are not those lamented by the writers who first drew attention to this trend. The actual effects of the large-scale organisation upon the middle classes are rather different.

Rather than pulling white-collar workers into an acquiescent middle mass, a principal effect has been fragmentary. Not all white-collar workers are allowed to share the advantages available in the world of the organisation. We have seen that more traditional sections of the middle class—small-scale businessmen and employees who come up the hard way—are not being totally replaced but simply squeezed. These groups are being left as a residual but persistent element within the middle class harbouring various grievances. And as we shall see in subsequent chapters, there are other groups of white-collar workers who are also being left outside and, in some cases, who are jumping ahead of the mainstream. The middle classes are being splintered. It is not just a matter of a new middle class replacing an older model. The older type is still around and is being joined by not one but several new middle classes.

7. The White Collar Proletariat

The proletarianisation thesis

Few people can be unaware of the growth of white-collar trade unionism in Britain during the last twenty years. This is now the fastest-growing section of the entire trade union movement. Today there are many white-collar occupations that are densely unionised even by blue-collar standards. For example, trade union membership is normal amongst teachers, bank employees and local government officials. There is no longer anything odd about the man in the white collar who belongs to a trade union. Until the early sixties, the growth of trade union membership amongst white-collar workers was doing little more than keeping pace with the growth of white-collar employment. Between 1964 and 1970, however, the proportion of non-manual employees in unions rose by almost a third; from 29 per cent to 38 per cent.[1]

Apart from the growth in numbers, white-collar unions have also been changing their tactics. They are now prepared to act in 'militant' ways once considered characteristic only of blue-collar organisations. Many white-collar unions no longer stand aloof but have affiliated to the Trades Union Congress (TUC), while, in addition to this, we have become accustomed to white-collar workers taking strike action, indicating a willingness to accept that relationships with employers involve bargaining and conflict. Old fears of militancy leading to loss of status and invalidating claims to professional recognition have been cast aside. Fifty years ago it would have been unthinkable for teachers or bank clerks to strike. In recent years, however, both groups have done so. So have town hall staffs, while civil servants in Whitehall have been involved in token stoppages. It would no longer raise eyebrows if it happened again tomorrow.

These developments are common knowledge. There is no dispute that white-collar trade unionists have been growing in number and that their organisations have become increasingly willing to use 'blue-collar' tactics. But why has this happened and what do these developments tell us about the white-collar worker's changing position in the class structure? These are controversial matters. One interpretation of the evidence suggests that former sections of the middle class are being proletarianised and assimilated along with the majority of blue-collar employees into the working class. Whilst some commentators have been arguing that advanced segments of the manual strata are prone to embourgeoisement, others have been alleging that parts of the white-collar labour force are being proletarianised and those who subscribe to this proletarianisation thesis attribute the process to a number of inter-related developments.

First, it is argued that vis-à-vis manual workers, the market advantages of some sections of the white-collar labour force have been seriously eroded. It is important not to exaggerate the extent of any such developments. Despite widespread beliefs to the contrary, the majority of white-collar employees are not lagging behind working class affluence. Nevertheless, there are undoubtedly some non-manual workers who are low-paid by modern blue-collar standards and who, in addition to this, have seen the relative value of their 'perks' eroded. For the manual worker, job security has improved as a result of the relatively full employment maintained since 1945, while, as a consequence of mergers and office automation, the threat of white-collar redundancy has loomed. Furthermore, the welfare state and trade union pressure have made paid holidays, sick pay and pensions into universal rights rather than white-collar privileges. As argued in an earlier chapter, on average white-collar workers still enjoy superior fringe benefits, but there are certainly some groups of white-collar employees whose market situations no longer clearly distinguish them from the working class.

Second, it is argued that many white-collar workers now face a promotion blockage similar to that which has always confronted blue-collar employees. In the large modern corporation there is a tendency to recruit individuals with degrees and other qualifications directly into careers leading to higher management levels, with the result that the man who starts at the bottom, in the office or laboratory, finds his prospects limited. Again, it is important not to overstate the extent of any changes that have occurred. Compared with blue-collar workers, on average white-collar employees continue to enjoy attractive career prospects and the 'ranks' are often filled by women who, up to the present, have not been expected to demand career opportunities. Nevertheless, there are male clerks and technicians in industry and elsewhere who are now finding that the bottom rung of the white-collar ladder has ceased to lead to any-where near the top.

Third, it is argued that shop-floor conditions are gradually being extended into white-collar work situations. Open-plan offices, 'pools' of clerks, and drawing-rooms where individuals work alongside dozens of similarly placed peers are replacing the traditional smaller bureaux with their intricate hierarchies. Hence, as amongst manual workers, it is argued that white-collar employees' work situations are increasingly encouraging an awareness of the difference between 'us' and 'them'.

No one argues that the above trends have enveloped the entire middle class. On the other hand, it can be plausibly argued that some white-collar workers are being overwhelmed by these changes and this is the basis of the proletarianisation thesis. It is alleged that as a result of deteriorating market, career and work situations, former sections of the middle class can be expected to regard themselves as no different from ordinary workers and therefore to identify with the working class, and one school of thought interprets the growth and increasing militancy of white-collar trade unions in these terms. Even if advanced sections of the working class are not being assimi-lated into the bourgeoisie, therefore, the authors of *The Affluent Worker*[2] admit the possibility of convergence with sections of the white-collar labour force that are being cut adrift from the middle class.

Are white-collar trade unions different?

Whatever its plausibility, some researchers who have examined white-collar trade unions have expressed reservations about the pro-letarianisation thesis. A number of writers have argued that white-collar trade unions are different; that like the leopard, even when he joins a union the white-collar worker does not change his spots.[3] The argument is that non-manual workers join trade unions not for 'working class' reasons but from distinctly middle class motives and, therefore, that their organisations retain a distinctly middle class character. A number of studies have suggested that joining a union does not necessarily imply that white-collar workers feel any soli-darity with the working class. Indeed, actual motives often involve a desire to stay ahead of manual workers rather than an inclination to unite with the working class to fight for a common cause. White-collar trade union leaders, on an ideological level, may share a great deal in common with their blue-collar counterparts. Union leaders representing all types of workers subscribe to a common 'labour' ideology,[4] but there is evidence that this consensus stops well short of the grass-roots.

In explaining why white-collar unions are different, reference is usually made to the individualism that is supposed to characterise the office, in contrast to the collectivism that is normal on the shop-floor. Traditionally if not always in the present, it is argued, their terms and conditions of employment have led white-collar groups to expect and actively seek personal advancement and promotion with a consequent rejection of the idea of pursuing group interests through collective action.[5] For this reason, the argument runs, density of union membership remains low amongst white as opposed to blue-collar groups, and furthermore, even when they become unionised white-collar workers' individualistic ideologies give their unions a middle class character of their own. According to this view, white-collar unionism lacks any ideological commitment to a trade union *movement*. Mercer and Weir[6] have claimed that the attitudes of white-collar unionists are distinctly pragmatic. If they feel that their careers are blocked they may turn to trade unionism, but they still retain middle class orientations. According to this school of thought, white-collar unions tend to be narrowly oriented, conservative interest groups, unconcerned with the pursuit of general social justice, more concerned with specific occupational interests, and preferring co-operation rather than conflict with management.

The *Reluctant Militants* study,[7] covering over 1100 technicians in industrial firms who belonged to a trade union, supports this line of argument. This study found that the technicians were marginal men, situated between management and the shop-floor without fitting easily into either group. But the group the technicians overwhelmingly identified with and used as a reference group was management. The technicians' problem, as they saw it, was that they were being denied their proper status and recognition. They were mostly ambitious and sought opportunities to move into management, and this was a source of frustration for the technicians found their avenues blocked. The majority of the technicians possessed paper qualifications, mostly from part-time study, but they faced a 'graduate barrier' since higher management positions were being filled by people with degrees and more prestigious professional qualifications. The technicians, therefore, regarded themselves as unfairly held down. There were complaints about traditional differentials—the technicians' superior earnings and career prospects compared with manual workers—being eroded. Expressions of solidarity with the manual labour force were conspicuous only by their absence. The technicians' concern was not to unite with the working class but to stay ahead of it. Becoming working class was what worried technicians rather than their objective. Hence the phrase 'reluctant militants'. The technicians had turned to trade unionism with mixed feelings. They realised that they were adopting a working class style of organisation and tactics and believed it was necessary that they should do so, but their feelings were ambivalent. They regretted being forced to become militant trade unionists. They had become organised like blue-collar workers, but not because they regarded themselves as working class. Their driving concern was to preserve what remained of their middle class privileges and status.

A. J. N. Blain's study of *Pilots and Management*[8] in the British airlines argues a comparable case. Airline pilots are in no sense an economically depressed group even by middle class standards, but trade union organisation amongst the pilots is strong. Furthermore, the pilots have been prepared to use the full weight of their bargaining power militantly and effectively. Indeed, Bain's research was designed to clarify what were felt to be the deteriorating industrial relations in the airlines. The results of his investigation suggested that what irked the pilots, drew them to trade unionism and disposed them towards militant bargaining behaviour was what they regarded as their declining status in relation to airline managements. The pilots in no way identified with the working class. They were drawn mainly from middle class backgrounds and their political orientations were overwhelmingly Conservative. They regarded themselves as an élite group of professionals—systems managers doing a technically complex job—and expected to be treated commensurately. The pilots' main grievance was that, as they saw the situation, they were not being accorded this treatment. As airlines have grown in size, pilots have become more isolated from top management and find it more difficult to influence decisions outside their aircraft. Bain's pilots, therefore, felt that they were being treated quite improperly as if they were merely workers. There were other irritations as well, including the insecurity that surrounds the pilot's job as a result of the regular technical and physical tests, and also the visibility of more highly paid foreign—especially American—pilots. Basically, however, the pilots regarded trade unionism as a means of obtaining the 'professional' rewards, recognition and status to which they felt entitled. Like the technicians whose militancy was reluctant, the pilots were adopting a working class means in pursuit of a distinctly middle class objective.

In studying bank clerks and their representative bodies, Blackburn coined the term 'unionateness' to clarify the differences between white and blue-collar trade unions.[9] Unionateness refers to the extent to which a specific organisation displays qualities that have conventionally been associated with blue-collar trade unions including a willingness to strike, and to affiliate to the TUC and Labour Party. Blackburn argues that while overall density of trade union membership amongst bank clerks has for a long time been high, this has been achieved only alongside a low level of unionateness, thereby offering further support for the view that white-collar unions are pale shadows of their blue-collar counterparts. Likewise in his research amongst scientific and technical workers, Prandy found that even when such individuals joined a trade union they often wanted the organisation to retain or develop professional characteristics such as encouraging study and publishing a learned journal.[10]

These results from British investigations are entirely consistent with the conclusions of Sturmthal's international survey of white-collar trade unions.[11] Outside communist countries and with the solitary exception of Japan where the whole structure of the trade union movement has unusual features, white-collar workers are consistently less likely to be unionised than blue-collar employees. In addition, white-collar unions are less likely to strike and nearly always remain structurally apart from blue-collar unions. In Britain, for example, they are not merging their identities and memberships with blue-collar organisations. White-collar workers join white-collar unions. Furthermore, although many non-manual unions are now affiliated to the TUC, Labour Party affiliation remains rare and throughout the world, white-collar unions normally remain aloof from the ideologically committed socialist movements that blue-collar unions frequently support.

International comparisons lend no support to suspicions that while there may still be a long way to go, white-collar trade unionism in Britain is part of a process that will eventually lead to the assimilation of many non-manual employees into the working class. On the above evidence, the polarisation that Marxist commentators have been predicting for 100 years, in which workers by both hand and brain will stand united, remains very much in the realm of wishful thinking. Far from signifying a new solidarity with the working class, the above argument suggests that white-collar unions are more frequently vehicles for maintaining non-manual workers' relatively privileged middle class positions. Just as blue-collar affluence produces an affluent working class rather than bourgeois manual workers, therefore, so it is arguable that denying white-collar workers former privileges leads not to proletarianisation but simply to a more militant middle class.

Trade unions and social class

One major source of confusion in the debate surrounding the proletarianisation thesis has been the article of conventional wisdom that
equates individualism with the middle class, collectivism with the
working class and regards these orientations as mutually exclusive.
However, in the earlier discussion of manual respondents' mobility
ideologies and educational aspirations we have already queried
whether the working class is as devoid of individual ambition as some
previous commentators have supposed. And looking at the same evidence from the opposite angle invites scepticism as to whether the
middle class is especially hostile to collective representation and
action. As the authors of a recent study of *Social Stratification and
Trade Unionism* have noted,[1,2] when the evidence is squarely examined the aims of both white and blue-collar trade unionists appear

Table 7 : 1

Employees' membership of occupational associations

	White-collar n = 204	*Blue-collar* n = 213
% in TUC affiliated unions	36	78
% in staff associations or other trade unions	11	2
% in professional bodies	20	1
% no membership	33	19

to embrace a similar mixture of individualism and collectivism, and
the results of our own enquiry endorse this conclusion.

Respondents in our investigation were asked to name any occupational associations to which they belonged and their answers, presented in Table 7 : 1 from which the self-employed are excluded, may
at first sight appear to endorse the notion that white-collar workers
are the less disposed to collective organisation. Within the blue-
collar sample 78 per cent belonged to a TUC affiliated body, whereas
only 36 per cent of the white-collar respondents were unionised —
less than half the manual density.

However, interpreting this relatively low density of union membership amongst white-collar workers as proof of an aversion to collectivism is unwarranted. Membership or non-membership of a trade
union is no valid test of this issue. First, account must be taken of
occupational associations other than TUC affiliated bodies. White-
collar workers have a range of organisations available for the pursuit
of collective interests. For example, membership of staff associations

and professional bodies was considerably higher amongst our white as opposed to blue-collar respondents and when such organisations are taken into account the proportion of non-manual workers shown to be collectively represented, 67 per cent, does not compare unfavourably with 81 per cent who belonged to an organisation amongst the blue-collar sample.

Second, some allowance must be made for the closed shop arrangement that operates in many manual occupations. All trade unionists in our sample were asked their reasons for joining and, amongst manual respondents, the most frequent explanation referred to the closed shop despite its illegality at the time of the enquiry (see Table 7 : 2). Those who believe blue-collar trade unionism to be an expression of working class solidarity would find questioning members about their motivations a sobering experience. It is not just that the majority of members are in no sense activists. Apart

Table 7 : 2

Trade unionists' stated reasons for joining a union

	White-collar n = 90	Blue-collar n = 168
	%	%
Closed shop	22	49
Ideological/ethical	11	8
Pursuit of specific occupational interests	54	38
Other	12	5

from this, amongst the rank and file expressions of solidaristic attachments are highly untypical. It is surprising how many members do not even know the names of their unions. For many members the trade union is rather like an occupational pension scheme; you have to join, you pay your dues and eventually become entitled to certain benefits.

Trade unionism is sufficiently traditional in many manual occupations to have become, in effect, a condition of employment, while amongst white-collar employees this type of inertia joining remains less common. The operation of the closed shop amongst blue-collar workers must exaggerate their apparent greater preference for trade union representation that membership figures indicate. In many of the relevant cases, 'closed shop' was probably the respondents' immediate reason for joining. Some would no doubt have become members in any case and it would be extravagant to infer that 49 per cent of the blue-collar members in the sample were reluctant unionists. Nevertheless, blue-collar vis-à-vis white-collar membership figures must overstate manual workers' apparent greater ideological commitment to trade unionism.

If respondents who explained their membership in closed shop terms are excluded and if all occupational organisations are taken into account, then white rather than blue-collar respondents can be portrayed as the more favourably disposed towards collective representation. While confirming that blue-collar workers are the more likely to belong to trade unions, therefore, our evidence does not support explanations of this in terms of any prevalence of individualism and consequent resistance to the principle of collective organisation amongst the white-collar strata.

To the extent that they were unionised, was there any evidence that white-collar respondents were carrying attitudes into their organisations that would give them a qualitatively different character compared with blue-collar unions? Were our non-manual unionists colouring their organisations with distinctly middle class attitudes so as to make white-collar unions different? We addressed a number of questions in order to probe this issue. As already mentioned, we asked all the trade unionists in the sample their reasons for joining, but on this issue the comparison between blue and white-collar responses was dominated by the much larger proportion of the former referring to a closed shop. White-collar members were the more likely to mention all the other reasons for joining that were coded. If references to the closed shop are discounted, however, the main impression is of instrumental motives predominating amongst both the white and blue-collar samples. Expressions of ideological, ethical or political commitment to a trade union 'movement' were rare amongst both groups. White-collar unionists mainly explained their membership in terms of pursuing individual or sectional interests, but if this is interpreted as evidence of individualism then blue-collar unionists are shown to be no less endowed with this attribute.

Respondents who did not belong to a trade union were asked their reasons for not joining and their answers are presented in Table 7:3. Amongst white-collar respondents there was a relatively widespread indifference to the entire subject—the issue of joining had simply never arisen, whereas more blue-collar workers were waiting to be pressured, maybe by encountering a closed shop situation. However, there were more objections to trade unions 'on principle' amongst the blue as opposed to the white-collar non-members. This evidence, therefore, hardly suggests that white-collar workers are especially opposed on ideological grounds to the type of representation that trade unions offer.

We addressed two 'forced choice' questions in order to probe our sample's preferences as regards trade union goals and tactics. Structured questioning is an admittedly blunt instrument from the point of view of assessing what people really think. However, although blunt, it is a legitimate approach in judging whether there are variations in outlook between two or more populations. First, we asked whether respondents believed that trade unions ought to pursue general social objectives (promote social justice) or whether they should concern themselves solely with the sectional interests of their members. We wondered whether white-collar unionists would prove the more inclined to define union objectives in narrow sectional terms, but as Table 7:4 shows, this was not the case. The white and blue-collar unionists gave almost completely identical answers. Second, as regards preferred trade union tactics, we asked members to choose between co-operating with management so as

Table 7:3

Non-members' stated reasons for not joining a trade union

	White-collar n = 66	Blue-collar n = 39
	%	%
Condition of employment	17	13
Object on principle	20	28
No union/not asked to join	23	36
Indifferent	32	15
Other	9	8

to produce bigger shares for all, and bargaining with employers in order to increase the workers' proportion of the cake. In this instance the white-collar unionists proved the more likely to favour co-operative tactics, but as can be seen in Table 7:4, 75 per cent of the blue-collar sample felt likewise.

Investigators seeking to test the embourgoisement thesis have sometimes worked with rather exaggerated notions about what constitute typical middle class attitudes and likewise, in testing for signs of proletarianisation amongst white-collar workers there has been a tendency to exaggerate the proletarian character of the typical blue-collar employee. It is as well to remember that very few blue-collar trade unionists are class conscious in the Marxist sense and that although unrest may dominate newspaper headlines, 60 per cent of manual unionists have never been on strike.[13] Furthermore, many blue-collar unions are highly concerned with differentials. Indeed, the craft unions' main historical concern has been not so much to unite the working class as to keep their members ahead of the less skilled. So when we find white-collar trade unionists who are concerned about their declining status and who hope to use trade unions as an instrument to keep themselves up the ladder, it is a mistake to imagine that this is a peculiarly middle class phenomenon. Both blue and white-collar unions contain instrumentally oriented members and, alongside broader socio-political objectives, seek to protect their own members' sectional interests.

Density of trade union membership amongst white-collar workers appears to depend upon exactly the same factors that apply amongst the blue-collar strata. Bain's evidence[14] shows that white-collar workers are most likely to join a union when substantial numbers of individuals doing similar jobs are congregated together in the

Table 7:4
Members' views on trade union goals and tactics

	White-collar n = 90	Blue-collar n = 168
	%	%
Goals:		
General 'social justice'	72	73
Members' sectional interests	28	27
Tactics:		
Co-operate with management in producing bigger shares for all	87	75
Bargain to increase workers' share of the cake	13	25

same workplace. In local government, banking and insurance, therefore, density of membership is high even when judged against blue-collar standards. Teaching, with over 80 per cent of all practitioners in a union, is one of the most thoroughly unionised occupations in Britain. In manufacturing industry, in contrast, white-collar unionism has made less headway. Even when there are large concentrations of manual employees in factories there are often only small complements of office workers and they tend to be splintered between different types and grades of employment.

A concentration of employees doing similar jobs always favours the development of trade unions. To begin with, it makes recruitment easier. It is difficult for trade unions to organise, collect subscriptions and provide a service for members who are scattered in small pockets throughout a large number of establishments. Second, concentration seems to arouse a perceived need for a trade union. With a number of individuals doing a similar job, a consciousness of kind together with an inclination towards collective action easily takes root and, in addition, in these circumstances individuals are likely to feel that they lack personal access to higher management and require some type of collective representation.

Bain's evidence also shows that if and when a trade union is 'recognised' by an employer for negotiating purposes, this gives membership a boost. Recognition makes joining a union appear an unequivocally legitimate step and also makes it possible for the union to start offering tangible proof of its effectiveness. Normally a take-off in membership growth is required before recognition will be offered, but some employers, including central and local government, have been more sympathetic than others to the principle of trade union recognition.

White-collar unions are encouraged by exactly the same conditions as blue-collar unions and, given favourable circumstances, it does not appear especially difficult for white-collar unions to recruit. The relatively low overall density of membership amongst white-collar workers, therefore, appears due not so much to non-manual workers being the more resistant to the principle, as to their circumstances of employment being less likely to offer trade unions the chance to organise and operate effectively.

Overall, the evidence suggests that both blue and white-collar workers, whether they identify with the middle or the working class, are willing to support either individualistic or collectivist action, or a combination of both, depending upon the strategy that best fits their situations. The relationship between trade unionism and social class is more complex than some previous writers have assumed and these complexities must be taken into account before the validity of the proletarianisation thesis can be assessed. As regards this thesis, the implication is that the evidence concerning white-collar trade unions needs re-interpreting. White-collar workers can join trade unions thereby endorsing the principle of collective action without their attitudes otherwise becoming any less middle class, while, at the same time, white-collar unionists who display sectional, instrumental and sometimes highly individualistic motives are less unlike blue-collar unionists than has been conventionally supposed.

The key issues in the proletarianisation debate concern whether some white-collar workers' market, career and work situations are becoming akin to manual workers' and whether their values and perceptions of their places in the class structure are ceasing to be middle class and becoming working class. Assessing the relevant evidence requires us to determine how middle class persons typically define their positions in the class structure, for false stereotypes of either working or middle class attitudes can only produce misleading conclusions. We have argued above that a propensity to collective action is not especially uncharacteristic of the modern middle class. So what are distinctly middle class values? When Lewis and Maude were discussing this subject, middle class values meant taking a pride in one's independence, particularly from state support, a desire to conserve one's assets, a belief in the virtue of saving, and the cultivation of tastes in high culture. Times have subsequently changed. This characterisation no longer applies. What are contemporary middle class values?

The new 'middle mass'

The most common variety of class imagery displayed by our white-collar respondents, though it applied in only 27 per cent of the cases, involved individuals placing themselves in a largest, centrally positioned 'middle class'. In the area where our enquiry was conducted, this rather than the 'prestige imagery' sometimes considered characteristic of the middle classes was the modal type of white-collar class awareness. To be middle class is no longer normally to think of oneself as part of an economic or social élite. The phrase 'middle class' is most typically used in its literal sense—to describe the common, average citizen who is positioned around the centre of the social hierarchy.

In terms of occupational status and income levels, respondents who assigned themselves to a middle mass emerged as the non-manual strata's Mr Averages. As Table 7:5a shows, they were found at all levels of white-collar employment, but were most strongly represented in between the extremes. Similarly their income levels clustered around the average for the white-collar sample as a whole. Members of the middle mass were also 'typically white-collar' in terms of their socio-political values (see Table 7:5b). Their views tended to be accentuations of those generally distinguishing white from blue-collar informants. For example, support for the Conservative Party, opposition to any extension of public ownership and feelings of trade unions being too powerful were particularly widespread. In terms of numbers, status within the white-collar strata and attitudes, therefore, there are grounds for treating the middle mass as the core of the contemporary middle class.

Middle mass respondents mostly saw their own class as lying between an upper class, usually considered the most powerful, and

Table 7:5

Corollaries of types of class imagery: white-collar respondents

	Middle mass n = 58 %	Proletarian n = 30 %	All white-collar n = 243 %
a) Socio-economic status			
Registrar General's social class			
1	10	3	16
2	55	33	50
3NM	34	63	34
Income			
£3501 and over	5	—	14
£2501–£3500	24	13	22
£2001–£2500	33	23	25
£1501–£2000	25	37	23
Less than £1500	13	27	16
Education			
Received some post-secondary education	75	57	68
b) Social, occupational and political attitudes			
% voted Conservative at last general election	81	62	72
% favouring an extension of public ownership	12	43	24
% arguing that 'trade unions have too much power'	79	63	66
% completely satisfied with job	60	33	50
c) Trade union affiliations			
Member of a trade union	49	67	38
Trade unionists' stated reasons for joining			
closed shop	15	25	23
ideological/ethical	4	20	11
pursuit of specific occupation interests	74	50	57
other	8	5	9

an underclass which was sometimes called the working class but more frequently designated using terms such as 'lower', 'the poor' and 'the unemployed'. By implication, at least some manual workers were normally included in the middle mass to which respondents assigned themselves. Like many of the affluent workers in the Luton study, middle mass respondents did not see any major cleavage separating blue from white-collar workers but considered the main bodies of both as belonging to a broad, centrally positioned class distinguishable only from the very rich and powerful on the one hand, and the extremely under-privileged on the other. Needless to say, middle mass respondents were aware of inequalities, of income for example, within the class to which they assigned themselves, but they recognised no basic ideological cleavages, divisions of interest or contrasts in life-styles.

Some commentators have combined the embourgeoisement and proletarianisation theses and talked about the coalescence of the main bodies of the former working and middle classes into a new middle mass. In an objective sense, we do not agree that this is the historical trend. However, there are certainly many white-collar workers who see the contemporary class structure in these terms and this image of society is just as likely to be real in its consequences as the proletarian view of a division between 'us' and 'them'.

The job attitudes along with the ways in which middle mass respondents described their positions in the class structure indicated an acquiescence in the secure and reasonably comfortable circumstances they perceived themselves as occupying. As described in Table Vb, middle mass informants were more likely to express complete satisfaction with their jobs than the white-collar sample as a whole. They appeared to regard themselves as firmly anchored around the centre of the class structure, disclosed few fears of being dislodged and similarly, displayed no strong ambitions to rise into higher strata.

For example:

I think there would be too many complications about being in a higher class. I prefer to stay where I am.

Needless to say, many middle mass respondents confessed that the idea of enlarging their incomes was appealing. It was rare, however, for even such individuals to seek social assimilation into a higher class:

From the financial point of view I think it would be rather nice to be in the well-off bracket. But I'm not bothered about mixing with a different type of person.

We have earlier rejected stereotypes that treat the working class as devoid of personal ambition. Likewise it is mistaken to regard the white-collar strata as uniform status-strivers. There are many white-collar workers who are quite content with their middle class positions and who have no desire to personally climb further up the ladder. As the Pahls found in their study of managers referred to in the previous chapter, the idea of settling on a secure plateau is a common middle class aspiration. Members of the middle mass may grasp whatever promotion and pay increments are offered, but have no fierce aspirations to join a more privileged class with different interests and social habits to those where they already belong.

The members of our middle mass were not 'organisation men' in the exact terms sketched by Whyte and Wright Mills. These creatures are purely figments of the sociological imagination. However, the classic portrait of the organisation man is misleading only in so far as it alleges that in the service of the corporation the employee loses his independence and suffers a loss of quality of life outside the workplace. The middle mass is a product of the growth of the large-scale organisation. It consists mainly of men who fill or hope to move into the solid central levels of management, public administration, banking and insurance—men who are building modestly successful organisational careers. Furthermore, as earlier observers have suspected, this middle mass is an amorphous body. There is little sign of collective cohesion amongst the white-collar strata's Mr Averages. The middle mass does not attract any strong feelings of group loyalty or generate collective societal goals. It is essentially a collection of individuals enjoying similar privileges and life-styles, rather than a class with a clear and distinctive sense of its interests and proper place in the world. In Crozier's terms, it is a 'class without consciousness'—a fragile base for any industrial or political movement.

Dennis Wrong has argued that it is possible to have inequality without stratification, meaning that a population can be arranged in a hierarchy without separate strata, each with its own group consciousness, appearing at different levels.[15] According to Wrong, American society as a whole has moved in this direction. The evidence we have surveyed relates mainly to Britain where the verdict of 'inequality without stratification' certainly cannot be applied to the manual working class. At the centre of the white-collar strata, however, amongst individuals who locate themselves in a middle mass, Wrong's description fits neatly.

Middle mass respondents displayed no antipathy towards the principle of trade unionism. Indeed, 49 per cent were union members, a higher proportion than throughout the white-collar sample as a whole. The distinguishing feature about these members' support for trade unionism, however, was the exceptional tendency to explain their membership in terms of furthering sectional, occupational interests. As we have seen, this type of motivation is far from unknown amongst manual workers. But within the middle mass this instrumentalism was barely tempered by any broader ideological commitment to a trade union movement. As other investigators have discovered, members of the middle class are willing to embrace trade unions when they find the tactics relevant to their own objectives.

White-collar proletarians and trade unions

We have already encountered one 'deviant' type of white-collar class awareness in which individuals consider themselves part of a compressed middle class, a form of awareness prevalent amongst traditional sectors of the non-manual strata. Approximately one-fifth of our white-collar sample identified with a compressed middle class and a further deviant minority (14 per cent of the non-manual total) subscribed to proletarian imagery, locating themselves in a largest, bottom working class. The white-collar proletarians in our sample placed themselves in the same class as manual workers and saw the sharpest cleavage in the hierarchy as dividing them from a more privileged and powerful group, usually named the middle class. In other words, the white-collar proletarians perceived the class structure in exactly the same terms as manual workers who subscribed to proletarian imagery.

In some cases, non-manual respondents associated themselves with the working class specifically because they regarded themselves as 'workers':

There's the monied people and royalty; folk like that. Then there's those who have to work—to work hard. That's the main difference; those with money and those who have to work.

In addition to regarding themselves as workers, however, many of the white-collar proletarians explicitly dissociated themselves from the attitudes and life-styles which they believed were common amongst other white-collar employees:

I'm in the working class: at the bottom. Which class you're in is an attitude of mind and I'm working class. It's my life-style and attitudes that count. I see the people I work with as middle class and I hope I'm not like them. I don't like their attitudes. They look down on people who work with their hands, and spend all their time worrying about holidays in Spain, getting an '1100' and so on.

In terms of socio-political values, the white-collar proletarians veered towards the type of outlook normally associated with the working class. As Table 7:5b shows, there was less support for the Conservative Party than in the remainder of the white-collar sample, but above-average support for extending public ownership and, particularly when compared with middle mass respondents, the proletarians were less likely to argue that trade unions have too much power. In general, as is common amongst manual workers, the white-collar proletarians regarded themselves as excluded from middle class privileges and were prepared to support both the political and industrial action necessary to remedy this situation. Their outlook was 'working class' in the full sense of the term.

White-collar proletarians, therefore, are not mythical creatures. There are thousands of them and they can be found in the exact circumstances that previous exponents of the proletarianisation thesis have identified. The proletarians in our non-manual sample were distinguished by their relatively depressed socio-economic conditions. They were typically employed in routine jobs at the base of the white-collar occupational hierarchy, income levels were below the average for other white-collar groups, and a relatively large proportion had received no post-secondary education whatsoever (see Table 7:5a). Furthermore, levels of expressed job satisfaction were exceptionally low. Proletarian outlooks were common amongst individuals who had entered office jobs immediately upon leaving school, but had never obtained the further qualifications necessary to climb far up a career ladder. They were also common amongst persons who had risen from the shop-floor to supervisory or lower management levels but were unlikely to move any higher. In these circumstances individuals may appreciate that they are not manual workers, yet at the same time realise that they are not sharing many middle class privileges. They may also find that they are paid little if anything more than ordinary workers and, furthermore, their jobs may offer few intrinsic satisfactions. The non-manual tasks that an office worker is required to perform need not be intellectually stimulating. Similarly, the opportunities that are available to exercise authority and assume responsibility in many 'salaried' occupations are minimal. Given such conditions, white-collar workers are liable to regard themselves as part of the working class. They are not a group that is merely prepared to use working class tactics in pursuing middle class objectives. There are such white-collar employees and many of them are in trade unions, but there are others whose values are emphatically working class.

Our white-collar proletarians were exceptionally likely to belong to trade unions. As can be seen in Table 7:5c, density of union membership (67 per cent) was almost as high as within the blue-collar sample. However, as already indicated, the proletarians were only a minority within the total white-collar sample and, therefore, although the proletarians were unusually likely to be unionised, the majority of the white-collar trade unionists interviewed did not subscribe to this type of imagery. This could be why previous studies of white-collar trade unionists have encouraged scepticism towards the proletarianisation thesis. What distinguished the proletarian unionists from others was the size of the minority giving ideological reasons for having joined. Only 3 per cent of the middle mass and 8 per cent of the blue-collar members accounted for their membership of a trade union in terms of a general principle. However, 20 per cent of the white-collar proletarians did so. Amongst white-collar proletarians, one finds the same kind of ideological commitment to a trade union movement that can be discerned amongst the more class conscious sectors of the manual labour force.

A marginal fringe to the middle class is not novel. Neale has noted that during the nineteenth century there existed a permanent reservoir of men from 'respectable' backgrounds who had mostly received a modest education to set them above the working class, but who lacked either the wealth, social connections, qualifications or talent to obtain secure positions.[16] According to Neale, over a hundred years ago this 'uneasy' or 'middling' class was acting as a social base for radical movements amongst which philosophical radicalism was the most influential. Although historical parallels can be drawn, however, the modern white-collar proletariat is different, and the crucial difference is that many individuals on the fringe of white-collar privilege are now abandoning the middle class as a reference group and identifying with the working class. The reasons why some non-manual workers are now siding with the working class are quite straightforward. Many white-collar employees are today finding that they do not enjoy any market advantages in excess of the blue-collar workers'. Their pay and fringe benefits like job security and holidays are ceasing to distinguish them from the blue-collar employee. It is not that they are against individual mobility on principle any more than manual workers, but many of these white-collar employees realise that, like manual workers, they have reached their career ceilings quite early in their working lives and that their future prospects, therefore, must depend upon collective effort. In terms of conditions of employment and life-styles, these white-collar proletarians recognise that they share more in common with ordinary workers than top management and professional people, with whom they have little personal contact either in or outside the work situation.

The proletarians were a minority within our white-collar sample, but a point requiring emphasis is that all the white-collar workers interviewed belonged to one of several minorities. While a relatively complacent middle mass type of imagery was modal, it encompassed only a minority amongst all the non-manual workers in our survey. This is why regarding the middle class simply as the opposite of the working class is a misleading over-simplification. It is now possible to identify a number of white-collar configurations of circumstance that foster several distinct types of class awareness. Approaches to explaining variations in class awareness amongst manual workers, therefore, need to be supplemented in order to come to grips with the images of society that exist within the white-collar strata.

White-collar images of class are the more heterogeneous. While there may be only one working class, there are a number of middle class images of society, the distinction between the middle mass and the compressed middle class being but one case in point. Furthermore, variations in white-collar images of society are not associated with the same factors that are most useful in accounting for variations in class awareness amongst manual workers. Variations in manual workers' images of society are most sensitive to the extent to which they are immersed in blue-collar social relationships along with the associated working class culture or, conversely, the extent to which they are exposed to white-collar social relationships and values. In contrast, white-collar workers' images of society are sensitive principally to individuals' positions within the non-manual hierarchy. This is not to say that white-collar workers are mostly conscious of exactly where they stand on a finely graded prestige ladder. This is an additional deviant type of middle class imagery that will be discussed in the next chapter. The above proposition is simply that the consciousness of the white-collar worker is highly responsive to his particular position in the hierarchy. For example, an awareness of belonging to a middle mass occurs amongst individuals comfortably positioned around the centre of the non-manual hierarchy, while seeing oneself as part of a compressed middle class is characteristic amongst those following more traditional types of white-collar careers that have led them to above-average status and earnings but who now feel that their positions are insecure. Proletarian consciousness arises mainly at the base of the white-collar ladder, amongst individuals in the more routine kinds of occupations on relatively low pay, and whose status is roughly on a par with that of the manual worker.

Within the white-collar strata, therefore, proletarian awareness is generated by distinctly middle class processes. What seems critical is being denied privilege relative to other white-collar employees. In this sense the sources are specifically middle class, but the type of consciousness itself along with its associated social and political

values does not differ from the proletarianism that is common amongst manual workers.
Current trends seem likely to accentuate the cleavages that our investigation reveals within the white-collar strata. The growth of large-scale organisations tends, on the one hand, to restrict career opportunities, authority and demanding work to the qualified, thereby leaving a white-collar proletariat to discharge routine functions in offices, laboratories and workshops, while, simultaneously, this same trend threatens members of the middle class who have earned their status in traditional ways—by entering a family business or by working their ways into senior positions by loyal and diligent service.

Following his Rhode Island study, Mackenzie concluded that the trends in America are towards a formerly more homogeneous middle class being splintered into several distinguishable groups. Mackenzie also argues that a splintering process is occurring within the manual strata enabling an 'aristocracy of labour' to be distinguished. Hence Mackenzie's verdict that, 'the situation existing earlier in this century when all economic and occupational differentials fell neatly away from the watershed of the blue-collar/white-collar line is no longer a reality'.[17] In Britain our interpretation of the evidence suggests that a sub-division of the working class is unlikely and that the actual historical trend is simply towards a decline in cohesion. Within the white-collar strata, however, our findings entirely support Mackenzie's conclusion. The days when it was realistic to talk about *the* middle class are gone. The trends are towards fragmenting the middle class into a number of distinguishable strata, each with its own view of its place in the social structure.

8. The New Radicals

How radical is the working class?

In Britain the political party supported by most middle class voters is called the Conservative Party and this choice of name helps sustain an impression that the middle classes subscribe to generally conservative values. The British middle classes, equipped with bowlers and mortgages, are conventionally regarded as suspicious of change. Maybe this regard has an historical basis and was justified at the time when Lewis and Maude characterised the English middle classes, but is it still valid? From the end of the nineteenth century until the nineteen-fifties there can be little argument that the working class was a major force for change in British society. Working class aspirations, articulated through trade unions and the Labour Party, encouraged the state to play a widening role in regulating the economy, thereby creating greater security at work for manual employees in particular. In addition, principally working class pressure led to a welfare state supporting otherwise weaker members of the community and providing legal, educational, health and other services, previously dependent upon ability to pay, as right of citizenship. In an earlier era, however, it was the entrepreneurial middle class that built an industrial society in nineteenth-century Britain. Times change, and there are grounds for suspecting that since the fifties society has been entering another watershed. There is evidence to cast doubt upon whether the working class is still a radical force.

Radicalism is a term that demands clarification. In this discussion it means a desire for change and a tendency to criticise rather than insist upon maintaining the status quo. In addition, it implies that the desired changes are not reactionary and intended to restore a golden bygone age, but progressive and aimed at moving forward to a better society. It follows, therefore, that yesterday's successful radicalism easily becomes today's conservatism. To what extent has this happened to British trade unions and working class politics?

Having fought to achieve free collective bargaining the trade unions have become its staunchest defenders. Meanwhile certain sections of the middle classes have been promoting a new and growing style of radicalism.

The majority of manual workers vote Labour and of the two major parties in Britain, Labour remains the more radical. But what does this prove? Today the leadership of the Labour Party is overwhelmingly middle class and on many issues, including public ownership, the radicalism of the Parliamentary leadership is only weakly reflected amongst working class voters. As seen in previous chapters, the working class is still a source of oppositional values, but this dissent is thin and incoherently spread. Furthermore, there are many issues upon which disaffection with existing social arrangements is now as widespread amongst the white-collar as within the manual strata. For instance, a nationwide survey commissioned by *New Society*[1] during 1975 found that only 33 per cent of non-skilled (DE) manual respondents agreed that, 'People in Britain have a big say in how the country is run', but the proportion of AB respondents agreeing with the statement was also only 33 per cent. Likewise only 19 per cent of the DE group felt that, 'The ordinary man and woman has an important influence on big decisions', but as few as 10 per cent of the ABs endorsed this proposition. Amongst the DEs 52 per cent believed that 'The big decisions are made by a small permanent group of top officials and politicians', but as many as 62 per cent of the ABs felt likewise. When studies amongst manual workers reveal considerable alienation from political processes, investigators sometimes imagine that they are tapping a specifically working class form of discontent.[2] In fact, however, dissatisfaction with the man in the street's ability to influence political affairs is equally prevalent amongst the middle classes.

There is a range of contemporary issues upon which the Labour Party in Parliament is more radical than the Conservatives but upon which, in the country, support for the radical stance is strongest amongst the middle classes. On immigration, race relations and penal reform, for example, if radical spokesmen in Parliament are required the Labour Party is the most likely source, but in the country the radical line is equally if not more likely to find favour amongst the white-collar as the manual strata. Nowadays the middle classes are supplying leadership and support for a series of radical movements concerned, for example, with civil liberties, prisoners' rights and child poverty. The relevant pressure groups may be campaigning for the under-privileged, but the campaigning is being done principally by individuals from middle class backgrounds.

This is a phenomenon that has attracted less attention than it deserves largely because it does not fit into conventional stereotypes of the social classes that equate the working class with radicalism and the middle classes with conservatism. This lack of fit is indicative of how the class structure is changing and how formerly orthodox ideas need revision. Of course, it would be misleading to create an impression that the middle classes are bursting with radicals. This is not true. As we shall see, on issues including those listed above, the radical stance is concentrated within particular sections of the white-collar strata. The intention in the following discussion, therefore, is to precisely locate middle class radicalism and also to properly define its character, for the term radicalism can encompass numerous ideas about a better society. As will become evident, the middle class radicalism that is currently surfacing is by no means identical with more familiar working class aspirations and is likely to push society in different directions compared with the course of change that was dominant during the first half of the twentieth century.

The significance of student unrest

One middle class milieu in which radicalism can be readily observed is higher education. Anyone wishing to find support for political ideologies to the left of Labour, Gay Lib, or equality between rich and poor nations is better advised to visit a university than a trade union branch meeting. The centre of gravity in the political climate amongst students is quite different from that prevailing in society-at-large. It varies from faculty to faculty, and in the social sciences the climate is more radical than elsewhere,[3] so in this type of company, individuals who regard themselves as left of centre in mainstream politics frequently find themselves cast as arch-conservatives. Some educational theorists have alleged that higher education is part of the modern state's ideological apparatus, designed to implant technical know-how and also values consistent with the maintenance of the status quo.[4] How wrong can you be! Students reading even the social sciences are an overwhelmingly middle class body. Approximately 70 per cent come from middle class families and nearly all subsequently enter middle class occupations, but in general their orientations are more radical than mainstream opinion in the wider society.

To understand middle class radicalism, it is informative to examine student politics, and we can do so in some depth because the late sixties was a period of student unrest. It was a lively time of marches and sit-ins which have continued, but subsequently in a lower key which has commanded less attention. When the student movement was at its height, however, as sure as night followed day all the major incidents were followed by books and articles explaining what had happened. A diverse literature was generated. Following the unrest at the London School of Economics during 1967–8, for example, participants on both sides of the barricades subsequently wrote their books, and the School's social scientists contributed a formal survey investigation.[5] For a period students replaced the under-privileged working class as the most studied section of the population.

Various accounts of student unrest were offered and it does not appear that any single explanation contained the whole of the truth, but rather that a number of simultaneously contributing factors all helped provoke the turmoil that swept through higher education across several continents. Later reflection, however, enables us to settle at least a rough order of priority amongst what at the time appeared equally plausible, when persuasively argued, cases. One argument treated student unrest as a symptom of adolescent strains, anxieties and neuroses. We were told that student rebels were immature, over-sexed and could be regarded as higher education's equivalent to the Teddy Boys. Dr Spock was alleged to be partly responsible for a permissively reared generation predisposed to rebellion. In rather more sophisticated terms, other commentators treated student unrest as a manifestation of inter-generational conflict.[6] A changing society inevitably accentuates the generation gap and the universities were believed to be experiencing an invasion by the youth culture. Traditional university values, many feared, were threatened by the permissive, fun-seeking hedonism of the rising generation.[7] Other analysts blamed the universities themselves. It was argued that these institutions had grown too big, impersonal and research-oriented. Students were seen as kicking against their treatment as numbers on computer cards and demanding a more humane education.[8]

All the above accounts may have contained a grain of truth, but in a balanced assessment they hardly stand up as major explanations. To begin with, suggested sources of unrest such as adolescent neuroses did not suddenly arrive during the nineteen-sixties but had been around for much longer. Equally seriously, the explanations listed above all completely ignore and do not even attempt to take account of what the participants in the student movement were saying.[9]

If they wish to be taken seriously, social scientists must treat their subjects' ideas similarly. When studying managers and how they run their organisations, it is normal for researchers to listen to what the managers say about how they are trying to organise affairs efficiently to operate their concerns at a profit. Investigators do not completely ignore these actors' accounts and proceed to relate managers' behaviour to their treatment in infancy. Research that proceeded in such a manner would not be treated seriously, and when studying delinquents, shop stewards or students there is an equivalent obligation to listen to their own accounts of their behaviour. The student activists of the sixties possessed ideas. They were not mindless rebels. Neither were they just playing games. They knew what they were about and to understand their behaviour it is necessary to pay attention to their versions of what they were trying to achieve. Analysts who adopted this approach have left accounts of student unrest that still make plausible reading.

One school of thought insisted that student unrest be treated as a manifestation of a broader protest movement.[10] During the nineteen-sixties, particularly in America, new issues arose to replace or at least rest alongside older grounds for conflict and dissent. There were specifically campus issues including the structure of university government and in addition, there was civil rights and the war in south-east Asia. These new issues were not accommodated into mainstream politics in that the divisions of opinion they housed did not initially correspond and were not assimilated to established party cleavages. Hence the radicals' stance, on the Vietnam war for example, inevitably included not only this emotive issue itself but eventually the entire political set-up. Given several such inflammatory issues the radicalism engendered could feed upon itself, encompass other topics including drugs and sexual ethics and become a generalised counter-culture involving a rejection of core features of western society, such as its technology and corporate character, and offering a vision of an alternative social order. This was never an entirely coherent and unanimously agreed vision amongst the radicals. Indeed, there were numerous Marxist, existentialist and other factions within the counter-culture. However, there was a common commitment to progress and, in contrast with more familiar working class radical movements, the students were not seeking for themselves privileges that their societies made available only to a fortunate few. Their values amounted to a genuine counter-culture and their vision was of an alternative society. They rejected even what ordinarily counted as success in the societies in which they lived. Hence Charles Reich's interpretation of the student movement as the beginning of a process leading to the greening of America and the advent of a new social order.[11]

Now that the unrest of the sixties has ebbed, it no longer sounds so plausible to talk about a new protest movement in which students and other young people are the vanguard, which is shortly destined to sweep society-at-large along. The unrest of the sixties caused a ripple rather than a revolution. Indeed, the radicals were always a minority even amongst students. When world-wide student unrest was at its height there was no incident that involved the majority of the local student population, including Paris in 1968.[12] At the London School of Economics, according to the results of a survey investigation, no more than 18 per cent of the students sat in at the School for one or more nights.[13] Throughout the sixties there were many students who were in no sense radical. On American campuses support for Students for a Democratic Society, the main radical alliance, was outshadowed numerically by membership of Young Americans for Freedom, a right-wing 'Goldwater' group. In disorganised situations—on the streets, in industry and in universities—minorities can appear to represent wider bodies of opinion than they actually do and this appearance can be sharpened by mass media coverage. Hence, during the sixties, student and radical became almost synonymous terms in the minds of many members of the public. Student unrest was a genuinely radical movement and amongst students the radical spirit was and still is stronger than in the surrounding society. To understand the events of the sixties, the committed radicalism of the participants must be appreciated. However, it was and still is mistaken to think in terms of this radicalism overwhelming the entire younger generation and society as a whole, or even the bulk of the student body.

The growth of the intelligentsia

A mistake in many instant analyses of student radicalism may have been its treatment as a new phenomenon to be explained entirely in terms of new situations and issues. Rather than a radical minority being a novel element, it now seems more likely that a situation during the sixties allowed this longer-standing minority to become exceptionally visible. New issues certainly arose, particularly the civil rights and 'imperialist' war questions, that troubled a wider public than agreed with the radical answers proposed by those who attracted maximum publicity. Hence the radicals were operating in a sympathetic if not wholly supporting context. Also during the sixties student radicals pioneered new tactics, most notably the sit-in, and for a time the universities and public authorities were unable to counter this tactic effectively. In several instances the authorities actually succeeded in mismanaging situations so as to arouse public sympathy for the protesters. Consequently student radicalism, an apparently new phenomenon, exploded into the headlines. What has happened subsequently? The student radicals have not disappeared. They are still around and given the right catalyst higher education could erupt again. What is different about the seventies is that the issues of the sixties have lost their edge, while the tactics that earlier surprised the authorities have been countered. So student radicalism has become less visible as it may have been before the sixties, rather than non-existent.

Apart from revealing that they were a minority amongst all students, studies of campus radicals also nailed the idea that they were reacting against conservative backgrounds. In terms of social class origins, the radicals proved not untypical students in general, meaning that they came mainly from middle class homes. Despite this, however, many had parents who were sympathetic to their children's radical values.[14] By no means all but a significant number of the radical students were expressing a tradition handed down through their families rather than rejecting the conservative values of their parents. Similarly the student radicals were not rising against the conservative values of educators with whom they were in direct contact. As already mentioned, radical students are concentrated in social science departments where the political climate amongst staff tends to be left-wing. An investigation conducted in 1964 found that 66 per cent of all British social studies academics voted Labour, while only 18 per cent supported the Conservatives.[15] Social science students rarely have the opportunity to react against Conservative lecturers. Rather is the reverse the case. During the sixties many university radicals found themselves amidst a supportive culture, illustrated by instances of left-wing academics supplying student activists with advice and even leadership.

The conclusion towards which this points is that a radical culture preceded the generation of students that erupted in protest during the sixties. That generation absorbed this culture and inflamed it with new issues and tactics, but student radicalism is not as new as often supposed. It existed in the nineteen-thirties and before, and follow-up studies of older generations have revealed that although muted, their radicalism is by no means extinguished with passing years.[16] Before the Second World War it was common to hear talk of the intelligentsia; an old concept more rarely employed nowadays and in its heyday more commonly used in mainland European countries than either Britain or America. The concept refers to people engaged in intellectual occupations, principally teaching and writing, which involve handling, developing and spreading ideas, and many pre-war commentators credited the intelligentsia with a special role in society. Compared with other middle class groups, the intelligentsia was seen as detached from day-to-day political and economic affairs and therefore capable of developing an impartial view of its society's predicaments. Inter-war writers including Karl Mannheim believed that intellectuals had a crucial role to play in mediating between different interests and pointing the way forward out of the prevailing political and economic chaos.[17]

That the intelligentsia has been more radical than other middle class groups of equivalent social and economic status has been long recognised and this has conventionally been attributed to its ability to take an impartial and disinterested view of social issues. Post-war social scientists, however, have been sceptical about the supposed detachment and impartiality of intellectuals. It has become more common to explain intellectuals' radical tendencies in terms of special interests deriving from the positions they occupy within the social system.[18] Unlike the working class, they are rarely deprived economically. Nor are they subjected to anything resembling factory authority relationships. On the other hand, they lack the direct influence upon affairs commanded by members of the middle class who are active in business and politics and therefore are not equivalently implicated in mainstream social institutions. Furthermore, compared with business occupations in particular, the value of intellectual activity has never been considered measurable by market mechanisms. Hence, in societies with market economies, although not personally deprived, intellectuals' values often involve dissent from procedures used to distribute privilege.

Whatever the explanation of the intelligentsia's radicalism, there is no dispute that this radical section of the middle class has existed for some time. In nineteenth-century Europe, political dissent and instability have been traced to this group. In Britain during this period the intelligentsia was substantially contained as a result of the opportunities available for approved radical activity in industry, politics and the Empire. Elsewhere in Europe, however, the nineteenth-century intelligentsia tended to be a disaffected element.[19] Set in this context, the student radicalism in the nineteen-sixties can be seen as carrying on a radical culture that has been nurtured within 'intellectual' sections of the middle class over many generations. And it is only when recent student radicalism is set against this antecedent tradition that its contemporary significance can be grasped.

Richard Flacks is one of the few writers to deal with student unrest in these terms.[20] He argues that a long-existent radical section of the middle class has been growing due to the expansion of higher education which is gradually widening the influence of the intellectual tradition. Occupational changes are also significant, particularly the growth of teaching and welfare professions that has enlarged the environments traditionally hospitable to radical intellectual values. The radicalism that was once confined to a small intelligentsia, therefore, has spread outwards and as professions that formerly recruited through on-the-job apprenticeship, such as law and accountancy, have moved towards becoming graduate occupations, the radical tradition will have spread still wider. According to Flacks, from being a small group, occasionally influential but incapable of sustaining anything resembling a mass movement, the radical intelligentsia is becoming a forcible section of the population, recent student unrest being just one manifestation.

The results of our enquiry fully support this interpretation. In Table 8 : 1 we have separated respondents who had been through full-time higher education and obtained a degree or equivalent qualification from the remainder of the white-collar sample. The size of the resultant group is not large, no more than 24 respondents, but the attitudes they expressed contrasted sharply with the general climate of middle class opinion.

The highly educated group was not consistently more radical than other white-collar respondents on issues where working class radicalism is noted. They were less likely to have voted Conservative at the previous general election and more likely to have voted Liberal or Labour and were less likely to complain of trade unions being too powerful. On the other hand, they were less unionised than the white-collar sample as a whole and less sympathetic to the idea of further nationalisation. Contrasts were most marked upon issues where manual workers were generally less liberal than white-collar respondents. For example, support for Enoch Powell's views on immigration and race relations ran at only a third of the level recorded amongst the rest of the white-collar sample, complaints about the police being prejudiced were almost twice as frequent, support for the re-introduction of capital punishment was only half as strong and preventive or reformative measures rather than tougher penalties were favoured as solutions to the 'crime problem'. The handful of irreligionists in the sample were also concentrated amongst the highly educated and qualified. As Kohn has argued,[21]

Table 8:1

Education and attitudes on socio-political issues (white-collar respondents)

	Received full-time higher education and obtained degree or equivalent qualification n = 24	Others n = 219
a) Working-class radical issues		
% voting at previous general election:		
Conservative	60	73
Labour	30	25
Liberal	5	1
% in favour of further nationalisation	21	24
% trade union members	4	34
% arguing that 'trade unions have too much power'	50	68
b) Other issues		
% approving of Enoch Powell's views on immigration and race relations	21	62
% arguing that the police are prejudiced against certain groups	45	25
% to solve the 'crime problem' favour:		
a) tougher penalties	17	48
b) preventive-reformative measures	48	27
% favouring the re-introduction of capital punishment	29	68
% religion: none	17	7

the security offered by a large organisation may help its employees to be independent and critically minded, but a radical and critical orientation is most effectively fostered by contact with the intellectual culture that is part of higher education, while a sense of independence is helped when individuals owe their positions to qualifications and education rather than their value in the eyes of a solitary employer.

The careers and life-styles of our highly educated respondents set them apart from other non-manual groups. As Table 8 : 2 shows, compared with the remainder of the white-collar sample they were exceptionally likely to be in our top income group, earning over £3500 per year at the time of the enquiry. In addition, they were exceptionally likely to express complete satisfaction with their jobs. Aside from its radicalising potential, higher education has become the route *par*

Table 8:2

Education and life style: white-collar respondents

	Received full-time higher education and obtained degree or equivalent qualification n = 24	Others n = 219
% annual income: over £3500	52	9
% completely satisfied with job	71	47
% always lived on Merseyside	54	65
% always worked in the same trade or profession	83	55
% no. of jobs held: one	46	29
% attended church: once or more during previous month	50	26
% member of a political party	17	6

excellence to both intrinsically and extrinsically rewarding employment.

The highly educated were more likely than other white-collar groups to have been geographically mobile since childhood. At the same time, they were the more likely to have spent their entire working lives in the same profession and 46 per cent had held only one job. Higher education sends individuals spiralling upwards but without their occupational careers becoming disjointed. The highly educated were also the main 'joiners' in our sample. Despite the concentration of irreligionists in this group, overall they were by far the most frequent church attenders. Furthermore, they were three times as likely as the remainder of the white-collar and the entire blue-collar sample to be members of political parties. This evidence suggests that leadership in 'community' organisations of all types is becoming part of the life-style distinguishing a highly educated, geographically and upwardly mobile section of the middle class that subscribes to an intellectual brand of radicalism, and the implications of this trend for society-at-large will be examined below.

The new radicalism

Frank Parkin is one of the few previous researchers to define the nature of middle class radicalism, his attempt following a study of members of the Campaign for Nuclear Disarmament around the time of its Easter march in 1965.[22] Parkin questioned 358 adult members along with 445 younger marchers and discovered that CND was an overwhelmingly middle class movement. Of the adults, 83 per cent were in white-collar occupations, but from particular sections of the middle class. They had mostly received a higher education and worked in the welfare or intellectual professions. Amongst the younger participants only 14 per cent had attended secondary modern schools. They were mostly in or proceeding towards full-time higher education, studying the humanities and social sciences. In other words, the young CNDers were social replicas of the adults only a generation younger and the profiles of both groups bore a strong resemblance to the middle class radicals within our sample. Parkin found that 62 per cent of the young marchers had a parent who supported CND, which is consistent with the findings of later research amongst student radicals—that their parents are often sympathetic rather than conservative-minded.

Amongst Parkin's sample support for CND was usually just one element in a more general radicalism. In addition to favouring nuclear disarmament, three-quarters were opposed to the monarchy as a social institution and 58 per cent were non-religious. They were radicals not merely on defence policy, but held views that diverged from statistically normal opinions on virtually every topic explored.

Parkin's analysis suggests certain contrasts between the type of radicalism displayed by his middle class subjects and the styles of working class radicalism that are institutionalised, for example, in the trade union movement. Two major differences are apparent. Firstly, Parkin's research suggested that for the participants, CND along with its marches acted as an expressive form of political activity, meaning that while the participants naturally hoped that nuclear disarmament would happen they did not really expect their campaign to have such an effect. Irrespective of this, however, they felt that the movement was worthwhile if only because it offered an opportunity to express their radicalism; not merely their support for CND but their radical feelings in general. This was psychologically satisfying and for the participants marching was to a large extent an end in itself. Compared with this, trade union activity is much more pragmatic.

A further contrast follows Parkin's observation that support for radical causes amongst his subjects was a matter of principle rather than interest. The participants in CND did not feel themselves to be a group that would reap special benefits if their movement achieved its objective. Support for CND was a matter of principle reflecting general moral and humanitarian values. This squares with the middle class radicalism displayed by the highly educated and qualified respondents in our enquiry. They could not expect any special personal benefits from a reduction in police prejudice, emphasising prevention and reform in penal policy, or liberal policies in race relations and immigration. Their radicalism was disinterested, which contrasts with trade union activity where a basic objective is to protect and further the members' interests. This should lead us to anticipate that in so far as middle class radicals are influential, the effects of their values will be different from the directions of change that have been promoted by the labour movement.

Within our white-collar sample, 15 per cent subscribed to a type of class imagery in which the social hierarchy was portrayed as a finely graded ladder. This type of imagery has sometimes been treated as the modal form of middle class awareness, but throughout our sample it was less prevalent than middle mass imagery and was common only amongst highly educated respondents who, as we have seen, tended to be of an unusually radical frame of mind. In 'ladder' imagery no single stratum was regarded as numerically dominant. Individuals who perceived the class structure in these terms usually described themselves as middle class, located their own stratum immediately beneath other layers of the middle class and above either less prestigious levels or the higher echelons of the working class. However, the terms these respondents used in describing their positions varied considerably, sometimes displaying a degree of 'sociological' sophistication. For example: 'I'm an A4; in the lowest quartile of the top group that market researchers identify.'

Other respondents located themselves in the 'professional', 'more highly' or 'more modestly' paid sections of the middle class, but the common theme was that the strata in which these informants placed themselves were not regarded as real groups with specific interests and clearly defined boundaries. It was more a question of these individuals locating themselves at a particular point along a continuous scale or on a certain rung of a ladder.

Individuals subscribing to ladder imagery overlapped considerably with the highly educated group whose values have already been discussed. They were more likely to possess professional qualifications and to be earning over £3500 per year than the white-collar sample as a whole (see Table 8:3) and presented the same radical skew across the same range of issues. Identifying the class imagery associated with this radicalism is important in order to understand its character. Very frequently, while admitting that a class structure existed and that they belonged to a particular class, these respondents made it clear that they found the subject rather distasteful. They felt no class loyalties. Indeed, several explicitly dissociated themselves from the types of class awareness they considered common amongst socio-economic peers. For instance: 'I suppose I'm in the professional middle class, but really I don't like to think there are classes at all. I am only in a particular class because others create classes. I would prefer everybody to be in the same class.'

Hence the relatively disinterested and principled nature of their radicalism. These respondents did not positively identify with and therefore did not wish to enhance the interests of any particular class. In terms of their career histories, the individuals who subscribed to ladder imagery emerged as the Mr Successes of the sample. As already mentioned, they were relatively highly paid and, as shown in Table 8:3, were more likely than the remainder of the white-collar sample to have experienced inter-generational upward social mobility. Their ascents of the social scale were typically based upon education and the acquisition of paper qualifications, and their perceptions of the class structure resembling a ladder to be climbed were

Table 8:3
Corollaries of 'ladder' and other white-collar class images

	'Ladder' imagery n = 32	All white-collar n = 243
% annual income of over £3500	25	15
% upward inter-generational mobility between RG's social classes	81	70
% members of a professional association	22	12

probably related to this experience. Their sympathies lay not with a middle class they were pleased to have joined, for they did not see their situations in these terms. Their views suggested a vicarious and inconsistent identification with the working class from which some had arisen, but in general their radicalism was not geared to the interests of any particular section of the community.

The non-manual strata are increasingly supplying leadership for a variety of radical groups. Middle class radicals are not only inspiring a range of pressure groups concerned with everything from the environment to poverty, but are also taking over leadership positions in what have traditionally been working class organisations and the policies of these organisations are likely to change accordingly. In the British Communist Party approximately a quarter of today's members are from the white-collar strata and Newton's research indicates that this middle class membership tends to favour an idealistic style of communism involving considerable interest in international affairs, whereas working class members are more concerned with 'mundane' matters such as housing and jobs.[23] In the Labour Party the Parliamentary leadership is now predominantly middle class, and at constituency levels stalwarts with roots in working class communities and trade unions appear to be giving way to middle class activists. Along with this there is some evidence of a shift in emphasis on agendas away from working class issues, particularly housing, towards a concern with matters of principle such as foreign policy and immigration.[24] There is no evidence that middle class activists in the Communist and Labour Parties are less radical or left-wing than working class members. The implication of the middle class take-over is not that these movements will shift to the right, but that their concern will gradually switch to different issues.

Table 8 : 4 and Table 8 : 5 summarise the main types of class imagery discerned amongst our white-collar sample. The largest minority

Table 8:4
White-collar class images

	Name of own class	*Number of classes recognised*	*Position of own class*	*Largest class*	*Position of largest class*
a) Proletarian	Working	2	Bottom	Own	Bottom
b) Middle mass	Middle	3	Centre	Own	Centre
c) Compressed middle class	Middle	3	Centre	Beneath own	Bottom
d) Ladder	Middle	4 or more	Centre	None	—

regarded themselves as part of a middle mass, while smaller 'deviant' minorities subscribed to compressed middle class, ladder and proletarian types of imagery. There were inevitably some respondents who did not fit tidily into any of these main categories. The views expressed by some informants were idiosyncratic or inconsistent and have been left unclassified. The only distinguishable type of white-collar imagery not discussed above covers instances where respondents described themselves as working class, but unlike the proletarians placed this class towards the centre rather than at the base of the hierarchy. The socio-political values of these respondents stood midway between the proletarians' and those subscribing to middle mass imagery and their occupational and economic circumstances were similarly midway. Rather than representing a discrete type of imagery, therefore, these cases seem better treated as an intermediate mixture.

It is desirable to re-emphasise that all images named above are ideal types towards one of which most respondents' views approximated. Each type contains many individual variations and in practice, instances classified under each heading shade into others. The manner in which we have presented our findings deliberately sharpens a more blurred reality. Far from distorting reality, however, the intention has been to identify real tendencies that are ordinarily less visible, most particularly the manner in which changes in the white-collar sector are having an all-round splintering effect within the middle classes.

Traditional sections of the middle class now feel threatened both by working class power and by the new competitors who have appeared in the higher socio-economic strata. These competitors include organisation men who fill middle management levels and keep the wheels of bureaucracy grinding and also the highly educated and

Table 8:5

White-collar images of class

	n = 243
	%
Middle mass	27
Compressed middle class	19
Ladder	15
Proletarian	14
Central working class	11
Other	14

qualified who owe their positions to certificates rather than service and connections. This latter group are men who realise that they belong within the middle classes but feel little loyalty to these strata and display definite radical tendencies. They gravitate to occupations in which their radicalism can find expression, principally education, but also other professions that recruit from higher education. Consequently the more conservative and acquiescent sections of the middle classes often feel let down and betrayed by people in positions where they expect to find support and confirmation of their traditional values. Hence the anger aroused by the alleged left-wing bias of media-men and distrust of higher education. Meanwhile, at the base of the white-collar hierarchy, other less well-qualified employees are being proletarianised by the overhead recruitment of the more highly educated.

Current trends can only accentuate the divisions that are already evident within the middle classes. The continued growth of the large corporation and the expansion of higher education can only further open up the divisions of interest and ideology that the evidence already reveals. Thirty years ago it may have been possible to speak of *the* English middle classes and to sketch a single archetype towards which all aspirants towards middle class status converged. Today this is no longer possible. The middle classes are fragmented. It is now possible to distinguish a number of middle class situations and outlooks—that of a solid and relatively acquiescent middle mass, proletarian white-collar workers, threatened and compressed traditional groups, and the qualified spiralists who espouse a radical liberalism. In the recent past the position of the working class has constituted the main threat to cohesion, and working class dissent has been a major source of social change with the middle classes playing a mainly defensive, conservative role. In the future, however, it is likely that the management of conflict between various sections of the middle classes with their different interests and values will be an equally arduous political task and that it will be these new lines of conflict that increasingly stimulate social change.

9. Politics in the Fragmentary Class Structure

Whether their members realise it or not, all societies have to solve a political problem—to avoid anarchy and maintain order and alongside evidence from the contemporary world, history amply demonstrates that solutions are not guaranteed by divine providence. How can men who are capable of independent thought and action, and who often possess conflicting values and interests, gain the security and comfort that require a generally observed framework of rules? Political philosophers have long been aware that solutions to this problem of order must wrestle with the implications of social inequalities. Some form of stratification may be unavoidable, but it equally inevitably generates conflict and consequent threats to order.[1] One answer lies in coercion, but the long-term effectiveness of crude oppression is debatable and, in any case, most of us prefer the liberty associated with a political system that operates on the basis of consent. In a free but unequal society, therefore, politics has to involve articulating, comprising and resolving the different interests that inevitably accompany a division of labour to the satisfaction of all the parties and the problem is to devise arrangements that will achieve this objective.

Throughout history hundreds of states have experimented with constitutions to solve their political problems. The only apparently permanent solutions have been the latest. Yet in western countries and maybe especially in Britain with its renowned tradition of political stability, during recent decades many have shared a comfortable belief of having discovered an ultimate solution called democracy. Who is against democracy? But exactly what do we mean by the term? A glance around the contemporary world shows that democracy means different things in different states. Rather than a set of political arrangements given and valid for all time, therefore, it may be more appropriate to regard the liberal values lying behind the term 'democracy' as requiring different types of institutional expression to handle the changing patterns of conflict that occur in changing societies. Even democratic solutions to the political problem may never be final, but merely a succession of temporary truces. Complacency in the face of mankind's political problem is never warranted even in societies that take pride in their democratic ideals and practices.

The western world has not only developed democratic political practices but has also produced a school of political scientists who have formulated theories explaining how western-style democracy offers an admirable solution to the problem of articulating, compromising and satisfying initially conflicting interests.[2] According to the theory, the key institutions in an effective democracy are elections on the basis of adult suffrage, political parties, with preferably only two dominating the arena, and parliamentary government. Elections are considered important in order to keep governments responsive to popular opinion and to enable the public's grievances and aspirations to be fed into the political process. Parliamentary institutions are judged important in order that governments should be kept immediately answerable to representatives of the people between more periodic elections. Finally, political parties are identified as playing a crucial role in articulating and compromising sectional interests and in presenting voters with realistic packages of policies that can be implemented if their party wins an election. This theory of democracy claims that there needs to be more than one party in order to provide the competition and incentive to keep governments responsive to the people. At the same time, however, according to the theory, it is desirable that no more than two major parties should dominate the scene, firstly in order to ensure stable government since in a multi-party situation it is likely that no government pursuing a coherent policy would be able to command a parliamentary majority and secondly because large parties must necessarily be coalitions which comprise a range of sectional interests within their own programmes, thereby developing similar moderate policies that will be tolerable even to supporters of the losing side.

Whatever its scientific merits, this theory expresses the ideals that defenders of western democracy claim that their preferred political arrangements embody, and many commentators have pointed to 'stable Britain' as a prime example. Within Britain, however, there are growing signs that the political system is ceasing to function as the theory suggests it should. The political parties are proving to be a weak link and during recent years three symptoms of political malaise have attracted comment.

The first symptom is the decline in the electoral support achieved by the two major parties during the last thirty years. Membership of these parties has been falling and so have the numbers of votes they attract at general elections. This has been partly due to a decline in turnout. The proportion of registered voters actually going to the polls at general elections in Britain has declined from around 80 per cent in the immediate post-war period to approximately 70 per cent. The election in February 1974, conducted on a new voters' register and amidst the feverish atmosphere of a coalminers' strike and the resultant three-day working week in industry, produced a turnout comparable to those of the immediate post-war years. In October 1974, however, turnout slipped back to its more recent norm of around 70 per cent. The decline in electoral support attracted by the Conservative and Labour Parties is further accounted for by the rise of 'nationalist' alternatives in Scotland, Wales and Northern Ireland, and in England by the re-emergence of the Liberal Party. Whether this latter trend indicates a resurgence of 'liberalism' is debatable, for there is evidence that the Liberal Party has been attracting a heterogeneous protest vote that can alternatively flow even to the National Front.[3] However, in total these trends explain how it was possible for the Labour Party to win the October 1974 election with the support of less than 28 per cent of all registered voters and this figure must call into question whether Britain's main political parties are any longer operating as broad coalitions that comprise a wide range of sectional interests and pursue policies acceptable even to their opponents.

A second symptom of malaise is the growth of civil disobedience. Of course, law-breaking by individuals has always occurred and organised campaigns for legislative change are not new. But recent years have seen a succession of organised refusals by otherwise re-spectable bodies to recognise laws passed by Parliament and antici-pated in the declared policies of the victors in the electoral contest. The most noteworthy instances have been the refusal of the trade unions to recognise the 1971 Industrial Relations Act and the refusal of several Labour-controlled local authorities to implement the 'fair rents' legislation enacted by the same Conservative government. Given this leadership from within the 'establishment', rent strikes organised by local, grass-roots bodies were probably only to be expected. Needless to say, the success of these campaigns—in each case the detested statutes were subsequently repealed—can only encourage repetitions. Earlier examples of civil disobedience in-cluded the tactics of the Committee of 100 in its unsuccessful cam-paign for nuclear disarmament and the successful attempts by anti-apartheid groups to stop the tours of white South African sportsmen. Irrespective of the merits of these causes, the tactics employed raise questions as to whether the political system in Britain is any longer ensuring that governments pursue generally acceptable policies and indicate willingness amongst the public to pursue objectives extra-constitutionally instead of relying upon mainstream political channels.

The third symptom of malaise comes from opinion surveys that have recently been revealing large sections of the public complaining that they have no effective control over their country's political institutions. Some of this evidence was presented in the previous chapter, showing that alienation from political processes is neither confined to nor even concentrated within the working class but is widespread throughout all sections of the community.[4] This evidence is hardly consistent with a theory claiming that the political parties ensure that all important sections of public opinion find their interests represented at the centres of political power.

So what has gone wrong? Why has democracy in Britain apparently turned sour? It is tempting to blame malevolent or incompetent politicians, but the real sources of malaise cut deeper and include the manner in which the class structure is being fragmented. As previous chapters have shown, at the grass-roots, patterns of loyalty and conflict together with divisions of interest have been changing while political institutions have not undergone any parallel re-alignment. The political system has not adjusted to the dissolution of traditional divisions and their replacement by a fragmented class structure. As a result, the political superstructure now rests upon shaky foundations and the entire democratic process is beginning to falter. It is important not to overstate this case. Democracy is not yet on the point of collapse. What we are describing is essentially a gradual trend. But if anything, this makes it all the more important to draw attention to a predicament that can easily be overlooked.

Fragmentary class structure is not the sole source of political strain in contemporary Britain. Other sources include demands for greater regional autonomy within the United Kingdom and the movement to develop representative political institutions within the European Economic Community. It is both possible and conventional to regard each of these issues as well as the symptoms of malaise listed above as entirely separate problems. The thrust of our argument, however, insists that it has become more realistic to recognise that the cumulative impact of these problems has made the constitution itself into an issue. Hence the current search for solutions in which proposals for electoral reform have ceased to be dismissed as the daydreams of cranks and have won a serious audience. Should Britain adopt a system of primary elections as in the USA, or proportional representation as in some other European countries? The political problem is universal, and people in Britain are now becoming aware that they share it.

The shallow anchorage of middle class political loyalties

The future of the Labour Party has been a standard issue in British politics for well over a decade. There has been continuous speculation on the implications of the decline in the proportion of occupations in the blue-collar sector coupled with what remains of the working class being whittled away by embourgeoisement. Hence every electoral setback has re-opened the issue as to the Party's future and Labour has become accustomed to handling well-meaning but embarrassing advice such as that it will need to change its traditional left-wing policies and image so as to appeal to a broader spectrum of radical opinion, or reconcile itself to a future as a permanent opposition. Meanwhile the Conservative Party has attracted little equivalent attention. Maybe the social sciences have not escaped the folk-view of the Conservatives as the natural governing party. That the more privileged strata, and certainly individuals who identify with the middle classes, thereby placing themselves well above the bottom rungs of the ladder, will remain a loyal constituency on whose support the Conservatives can rely, is a proposition rarely considered worth questioning. Radical intellectuals and white-collar proletarians have rarely been treated other than as deviant minorities dispersed around the middle classes' solid core. However, this solid core has previously remained largely free from systematic investigation and close scrutiny suggests that the core may be less solid and numerous than has been commonly supposed. To what extent does the Conservative Party still speak for the middle classes?

In our investigation, apart from asking respondents which political parties they voted for, we addressed a series of questions to discover how securely their party loyalties were anchored. We queried whether they had ever voted for a different party to the one supported at the previous general election and also asked whether respondents' wives and parents shared their party preferences. A history of political consistency is known to favour a consistent future[5] and similarly, it is established that individuals' political attitudes are liable to be influenced by others with whom they associate, one instance being that deviations from social class norms in voting behaviour are less frequent when individuals live in areas containing few representatives from other classes.[6] In addition we probed the nature of respondents' ideological attachments to their political parties and distinguished between those giving 'positive' and 'negative' reasons when asked why they had voted for their chosen parties. The majority explained their political choices in positive terms, stating that they supported their party's declared policies or believed that the party in question represented their particular sectional interests. Other respondents, however, explained their voting behaviour solely in terms of being against another party's policies, leaders or supporters.

The answers received to these questions are summarised in Table 9:1 with the sample broken down by occupational class and preferred political party. The evidence indicates, in general, that Conservative

Table 9:1

Anchorage of party political loyalties

	White-collar		Blue-collar	
	Conservative n = 142	Labour n = 51	Conservative n = 49	Labour n = 117
% always voting for same party	64	74	54	86
% whose wife votes for same party	61	45	53	60
% whose parents both vote(d) for same party	51	64	42	50
% with 'positive reason' for party choice	61	84	69	90

support is less securely anchored than support for Labour. Within the blue-collar strata, on all the indicators the prognosis favours greater stability for the Labour vote, while within the white-collar strata the deviant voters, in this case the Labour supporters, appear not less but more firmly attached to their party than those voting in accordance with the class norm. White-collar Labour voters were the less likely to have wives with similar loyalties, but were more likely than Conservatives to have parents with the same preference, to have always voted for the same party and to explain their support in positive terms. Within our sample and according to our measures, therefore, the party loyalties of working class Conservatives appear especially unreliable, while white-collar Conservative support does not exhibit anything approaching the solidity characteristic of the blue-collar Labour vote.

Society is becoming increasingly bourgeois in that a growing proportion of all occupations are in the white-collar or middle class sector. Talk about the diminishing working class, however, often overlooks some inevitable implications of expansion for the character of the middle classes. Expanding layers in the white-collar strata can only be filled by upward mobility, that is, by recruiting individuals from working class backgrounds and the volume of upward mobility has been accentuated in Britain as in other European countries by an inflow of immigrants into the least prestigious jobs.[7] Within our sample, 43 per cent of the white-collar respondents had been upwardly mobile from the blue-collar strata, whereas only 17 per cent of manual workers' fathers held white-collar jobs. These figures

Table 9:2
Social mobility and voting behaviour

	Social classes 1–2–3–NM		Social classes 3–4–5–M	
	Upwardly mobile n = 94	*Non-mobile* n = 125	*Downwardly mobile* n = 37	*Non-mobile* n = 181
	%	%	%	%
Party voted for at previous (1970) general election:				
Conservative	63	82	50	25
Labour	35	17	50	73
Other	2	1	—	2

will not exactly mirror the situation throughout society at large, but the existence of a higher proportion of middle class adults with blue-collar origins than working class adults from white-collar backgrounds is representative of the general situation.

As noted on many previous occasions, upwardly mobile persons are more likely to adopt the political norms of the strata they join than the downwardly mobile. Within our sample, therefore, as Table 9:2 shows, individuals who had descended into the blue-collar strata were more likely to vote Conservative (50 per cent) than were the upwardly mobile to vote Labour (35 per cent). However, as already pointed out, the upwardly mobile outnumbered the downwardly mobile and Conservative support was less prevalent amongst upwardly mobile white-collar respondents than amongst those born into their strata (63 per cent and 82 per cent).

Butler and Stokes[8] have observed that the Labour Party is only just beginning to benefit fully from the tendency for party loyalties to be handed down through the family. As a major alternative in British politics Labour is still a sufficiently recent arrival to be yet awaiting the full benefit that can accrue from children 'inheriting' their parents' loyalties. Since the blue-collar strata, the main source of the Labour vote, are now largely replenished from within their own ranks, this means that while the working class may be contracting in total size, its remaining members' own occupational situations and family histories will normally reinforce each other's influence towards support for the Labour Party and even if solidaristic party attachments are waning there is still no alternative political party that has developed a definite working class appeal. Hence the relatively secure anchorage of Labour support within the blue-collar strata.

The volume of upward mobility, in contrast, results in a larger part of the Conservative's traditional constituency, the white-collar strata, being exposed to cross-pressures and consequently its middle class voters' attachments to the Conservative Party are often shallow. Furthermore, the principal theme developed in previous chapters has suggested that the new white-collar strata comprise an economically and occupationally heterogeneous body, that a related process of ideological fragmentation is occurring and our evidence suggests that this trend is also helping to undermine the middle classes' instinctive and loyal conservatism. Middle mass imagery was the most common form of class awareness exhibited by our white-collar respondents and, as seen in chapter seven, those subscribing to it were more conservative in terms of their socio-political attitudes than other non-manual groups. The impression of this middle mass as the white-collar strata's solid conservative core is confirmed in Table 9 : 3 where their political loyalties are shown to be the most firmly anchored. The insecure anchorage of white-collar party loyalties compared with blue-collar respondents' was concentrated amongst the deviant minorities that collectively accounted for the majority of the white-collar sample—those possessing proletarian outlooks, regarding themselves as a compressed middle class, and subscribing to ladder imagery. If we can anticipate that the growth of higher education and the expansion of the professions will increase the prevalence of ladder imagery and its associated radicalism, simultaneously leading to traditional sections of the middle class feeling threatened, and also blocking the career opportunities open to individuals on the bottom rungs of the white-collar hierarchy, thereby encouraging them to see their situations in proletarian terms, the white-collar strata's solid conservative core seems destined to be further whittled away and the political loyalties of the middle classes are likely to become increasingly fickle.

While involving some extrapolation the above comments are more than speculation, and to emphasise the reality of the situation under discussion it is worth referring to the relationship between age and voting behaviour. The character of this relationship is well known, but remains worthy of comment. Our investigation yielded the conventional finding that the older age groups were the more likely to vote Conservative and the least likely to vote Labour (see Table 9:4). There are processes probably inextricably related to ageing and the associated changes in individuals' positions in society that dispose

Table 9:3

Class images and the anchorage of party loyalties

	Middle mass n = 58	Ladder n = 32	Compressed middle class n = 40	Proletarian n = 30
% voting Conservative at previous (1970) general election	81	59	72	62
% with 'positive' reasons for party choice	74	50	63	71
% always voting for same party	73	52	54	63
% where parents voted for same party	60	30	38	31
% whose wife voted for same party	55	42	61	41

attitudes to shift towards the right. Although the general trend was in the same direction, within our sample the connection between age and party preference varied between the white and blue-collar strata. Amongst manual respondents the rightward shift occurred only in the forty-five-plus age group, that is, amongst those born in the period when the Labour Party was unable to benefit fully from the tendency for party loyalties to be transmitted through the family. In future years, therefore, the growth of Conservative support amongst older blue-collar workers may subside. Within the white-collar sample, the rightward shift was sharper and began earlier, around age thirty, and amongst younger middle class voters Conservative support only slightly outweighed support for the Labour Party.

There is no reason to believe that the young middle class Labour voters covered in our enquiry will not become more conservative as they age and increasingly benefit from the privileges that a white-collar career can offer. However, the fact is that the Conservative Party needs positively to win support from voters upon whose loyalty it cannot depend at the beginning of their political careers. The family and educational backgrounds together with the economic and work situations of many white-collar employees no longer conspire to make the Conservative Party a natural choice. Their loyalties are often not securely attached to any party and although especially with advancing age the majority are continuing to vote Conservative. with many it is only because they regard this party as the lesser evil.

Previous research has shown that individuals who assign themselves to a middle class are less likely than working class persons

Table 9:4
Age and voting behaviour

	White-collar			Blue-collar		
	Date of birth			Date of birth		
	1942 and since n = 34	1927–41 n = 67	Before 1927 n = 96	1942 and since n = 22	1927–41 n = 64	Before 1927 n = 83
	%	%	%	%	%	%
Party supported at previous (1970) general election:						
Conservative	53	81	73	23	22	36
Labour	47	18	24	77	77	61
Other	—	1	3	—	1	3

to explain their party preferences in class terms and from this evidence Webb infers that although members of the white-collar strata may obligingly identify with a class when prompted in an interview situation, otherwise class is not an important frame of reference in their everyday lives.[9] For the middle classes, this argument runs, class is not as salient a feature of their social worlds as within the working class. Our investigation yielded comparable findings to Webb's in that 33 per cent of blue-collar workers but only 14 per cent of white-collar respondents replied in 'class' terms when asked to explain their party preferences. However, rather than seeing this as evidence that class lacks salience especially within the white-collar strata the sum of the data from our enquiry suggests an alternative explanation.

In the course of each interview, some time after respondents had completed their accounts of the shape of the class structure, they were asked which class or other social group within contemporary society they considered the most powerful and answers were coded according to whether or not respondents re-introduced the concepts they had previously spontaneously employed in presenting their images of the class structure. Only 16 per cent of the blue-collar respondents failed to describe the distribution of power in terms of the models they had previously outlined and only 19 per cent of the white-collar respondents failed to do so, suggesting that middle class awareness can be triggered other than when individuals are unambiguously invited to discuss the subject and that the types of class imagery that our enquiry discerned can operate as stable rather than completely transient frames of reference for the individuals concerned. The failure of the white-collar strata to explain their voting behaviour in class terms, therefore, may not be due to class being an unimportant category in their day-to-day modes of thought, but to the existing political alternatives being incongruent with the new middle classes' conceptions of their interests and positions in society.

The Labour Party has problems of its own that we will spotlight shortly, but at least Labour can rely upon a traditional vote which is still almost automatically delivered. This is a vote that the Labour Party can lose, but in the first instance it does not need to be positively won. The Conservative Party's problems are less publicised, but on balance, its predicament is no more comforting than Labour's. The strata offering the Conservatives dependable support are being enlarged, thus supplying a growing constituency to which the Party can appeal. However, patterns of recruitment into these strata, along with changes in the economic and occupational situations encompassed, mean that the Conservative Party's continued appeal to its traditional constituency must be considered problematic. As they have done in the past, the Conservatives may prove capable of maintaining an appeal across the white-collar strata, but the outcome of this task is as uncertain as the future of the Labour Party.

The several new middle classes that our investigation has identified share little in common. They all deviate from the more orthodox conservatism of the middle mass, but in entirely different ways. Except by picking up a diverse 'protest' vote, therefore, it is difficult to conceive any alternative political movement attracting all the middle class support that is currently insecurely anchored to the Conservative Party. Likewise, however, there is no obvious way in which the Conservatives could re-vamp their policies so as to kindle enthusiasm throughout the white-collar strata.

It must be stressed that the situation under discussion is not merely the Conservative Party's problem. It is an issue meriting wider concern because the general health of the political system depends upon the public's aspirations and discontents being successfully filtered into the political process. The weaknesses that are apparent in the Conservative Party's electoral base are indicative of the alienation of many sections of the contemporary middle classes from mainstream politics. This is not to suggest that a middle class revolutionary movement is imminent. The cleavages that our survey reveals within the white-collar strata remain covert and far from institutionalised. These divisions are not yet fully embedded in individuals' minds. Our several middle classes are barely conscious of each other's existence. As yet there are no occupational organisations such as trade unions clearly mirroring these cleavages, they are not reflected in the party political system and no sections of the political élite espouse ideologies definitely appealing to any of the deviant middle classes that we have identified. Not even the vocabulary available for individuals to use in describing how they see the class structure enables white-collar workers to locate themselves unambiguously. The existing language of stratification virtually restricts individuals to identifying with either a working or a middle class, thereby concealing underlying differences. As our enquiry has shown, a term such as 'middle class' can possess several meanings, yet the vocabulary allows individuals to do little more than add qualifying phrases such as 'lower' or 'upper' when locating themselves in the social hierarchy. Similarly the available range of political alternatives still tends to conspire to oblige voters to support either the Conservative or the Labour Party.

In the case of the working class a cleavage has become institutionalised in ways that, as we shall confirm, have largely ceased to reflect grass-roots opinion. Within the white-collar strata a different but equally unstable situation has arisen. Cleavages exist which are as yet neither institutionalised nor fully visible even to the sections of the public directly involved.

The erosion of working class institutions

The state of the working class is a topic of almost habitual sociological concern. In contrast with middle class dissent, it cannot be said that commentators have overlooked the threat to cohesion posed by the working class. No matter which dimension of inequality is selected—housing, income, power or educational opportunity—the subordinate status of the blue-collar worker is readily apparent and the potential for dissent is evident. Members of the working class not only possess problems but pose them for others and this has lent impetus to studies of blue-collar workers.

Sociologists have never found it difficult to understand why blue-collar workers should be critical of existing social arrangements and prepared to support radical movements. Indeed, the more perplexing question has concerned why the social system has not already collapsed or undergone radical transformation as a result of working class dissent. Three different answers to this question have been offered, combined in various ways by different writers, and the current state of the argument concerns not so much which one answer is right, but which combination and order of priority is most appropriate.

One school of thought stresses that collapse remains imminent, that the apparent stability of capitalist society is fragile and ready to be shattered by any crisis. We sketched this point of view in chapter five and added the many necessary qualifications. Throughout the century during which its imminent collapse has been constantly predicted, industrial capitalism has displayed an enduring quality that continues to require explanation. An industrial working class has now existed for too long for its integration within capitalist society to be dismissed as a merely temporary interlude. As argued in chapter five, although in principle it remains a possibility, there is no likely configuration of circumstances that will polarise the working class into a revolutionary force. A number of writers have pointed to grounds for suspecting that the working class could respond to a militant ideological appeal, and that the middle-of-the-road policies espoused by trade union and Labour Party élites throughout most of the twentieth century will have tended to inhibit rather than sharpen working class consciousness.[10] However, there are even firmer grounds for suspecting that a marked shift to the left by the labour movement's élites would only widen the gulf that already separates them from the majority of manual workers. Surveys of working class opinion including the evidence from our own enquiry all show that the typical manual workers' socio-political attitudes are less rather than more radical than the policies of the Labour Party and trade unions. It cannot, therefore, be only the absence of appropriate leadership that is restraining the workers' revolutionary potential. Additional explanations are required. What can be generally agreed, however, is that the working class remains far from totally quelled into acquiescence.

A second answer to the question as to how blue-collar dissent is contained stresses an ideological hegemony maintained by superordinate strata and thereby explains why the working class response to a revolutionary clarion-call would be less than whole-hearted. As the evidence reviewed in chapter five demonstrates, there is some validity in this view, though there are additional impediments to class consciousness that are not imposed from above. But as also argued, hegemonic values do not and cannot possess a total hold since manual workers' everyday experiences inevitably provoke conflict and dissent, and other mechanisms of social control are therefore required to support ideological apparatuses.

The third answer, which supplies the otherwise missing link, stresses the importance of the institutionalisation of dissent, arguing that class conflict has been channelled into institutions through which change can be accomplished peacefully, by evolution rather than revolution. The key institutions held responsible for managing working class dissent in Britain are the trade unions and the Labour Party. By articulating, co-ordinating and gradually realising working class aspirations, it is claimed that these organisations enable older types of class warfare and ideological confrontations in the political arena to be averted, while in industry it is alleged that the strike can wither away to be replaced by peaceful bargaining and negotiations.[11]

As already acknowledged, each of the above arguments has something of validity to say about the contemporary working class. There is scope for debate about which processes deserve particular stress, but for present purposes the object of distinguishing these arguments is that, when separated, they offer a framework within which the consequences of current changes can be assessed and the ways in which the contemporary situation of the working class poses a threat to order can be identified.

To begin with, there is no evidence of developments liable to provoke a revolutionary situation. This is not the type of threat posed by the present-day working class. Secondly, neither is there evidence that the ideological hegemony of superordinate strata is slackening. The contemporary threat to order derives essentially from a weakening of the institutions hitherto relied upon to manage working class dissent. The institutions in question, the Labour Party and the trade unions, still exist and on the surface may appear virile. However, two trends are conspiring to undermine their effectiveness.

First, leadership positions in the Labour movement, especially in the Labour Party, are fast being taken over by individuals from radical sections of the middle classes whose location and values were discussed in the previous chapter. This trend is not making the Labour Party any less radical. Indeed, since the nineteen-fifties if anything its policies have swung to the left. It means, however, that the

brands of radicalism being adopted by the Labour Party, on comprehensive education, race relations and sex discrimination for example,
are often no longer attuned to distinctly working class sentiments.
It would be wrong to give the impression that the Labour leadership has entirely lost touch with the working class. One does not
have to look far to find recent examples of Labour governments
realising working class aspirations initially articulated through the
Party's conference and through its contacts with the trade unions.
The repeal of the Conservatives' Industrial Relations Act and the
subsequent Employment Protection Act that the 1974 Labour
government introduced are prime illustrations, another being the
solidarity of the Labour movement following the Clay Cross affair
in which a Labour-controlled local authority persistently refused to
raise council house rents as required by the 1970–4 Conservative
government. As pointed out in chapter two, many working class
families' household budgets and housing prospects continue to depend substantially upon council house building and rent policies.
Hence the powerful emotions that Clay Cross came to symbolise.
These emotions were barely comprehensible to many middle class
observers to whom the relevant issues were matters of principle
rather than interest—fair rents and the rule of law. While this middle
class definition of the situation was not entirely foreign amongst the
Labour Party in Parliament, the leadership not only repealed the
detested legislation but substantially relaxed the penalties to which
the errant councillors otherwise stood liable. The Labour Party is
still an important vehicle for articulating working class aspirations,
but the point nevertheless holds, that some of its leadership's radical
stances do not reflect popular blue-collar sentiments. There are
further recent illustrations of the Labour leadership being painfully
reminded of how adrift from grass-roots thinking its policies can
become. The 1966–70 Labour government's experiments with a
statutory incomes policy represent one case in point,[12] as does the
debacle that involved proposals for the reform of industrial relations
being first introduced then withdrawn in the face of trade union
pressure. It is not only the country but also the Labour Party leadership that now needs an explicit social contract to ensure that its
policies are acceptable amongst its own supporters.
    A Trades Union Congress–Labour leadership link can help keep
the Labour Party responsive to working class sentiments, but this
strategy confronts a second contemporary development that is
undermining the effectiveness of working class institutions. This is
the trend, which is affecting the trade unions as seriously as the
Labour Party and which was discussed in chapter three, away from

manual workers leading lives encapsulated within tightly knit networks of blue-collar social relationships that foster sharply defined forms of proletarian awareness. The trends away from proletarian solidarity are not towards embourgeoisement, simply towards less precisely focused types of working class awareness, but with no less profound implications for working class organisations.

One consequence is that few manual workers feel any inclination or obligation to participate in working class institutions. At the grass-roots, working class activists in the Labour Party are often in embarrassingly short supply.[13] The middle class take-over has required few pitched battles. Likewise attendances at trade union branch meetings are notoriously thin. Another symptom of this absence of solidarity concerns the number of manual workers who no longer associate themselves and their interests with the actions of their nominal representatives. A prime example is the widespread suspicion of trade union power. These suspicions are undoubtedly encouraged by the media and other channels for hegemonic values, but they are also nurtured by the fact that rank-and-file members know how little influence they exercise upon trade union leaders' policies and actions. Hence the situation, described in the *New Society* survey quoted in the previous chapter,[14] in which only 3 per cent of a national sample listed trade union leaders as amongst those whose opinions they would pay attention to when making up their minds about the desirability of Britain's continued membership in the European Economic Community.

In any social contract with the government, there can be little confidence in trade union leaders' ability to guarantee the compliance of their members. Unlike company directors, trade union officials lead only by consent and they have been increasingly discovering that they cannot always rely upon the loyalty and solidarity required to keep their armies organised. For the Labour Party leadership, the predicament is one in which it can placate working class activists by pursuing policies endorsed by the trade unions and also by the Labour Party in the country. But many workers today in no way identify with these working class institutions. In our sample there were more blue-collar Labour voters who favoured trade union power being curbed than increased and, likewise, not all working class voters have a vested interest in subsidising council house tenants.

With both the Labour Party and the trade unions, there is no immediate danger that their blue-collar members will desert. Nevertheless, the social foundations of the unions and the Labour Party are being eroded by the trends outlined above. A product of these trends is the growing disorganisation of working class dissent, symptoms of which include the proportion of strikes that are now unofficial, the level of non-participation in trade union affairs, and non-voting, particularly in local government elections. The net result is that working class élites are left incapable of engendering the support required to execute policies that would deal effectively with problems such as wage-cost inflation and this situation is a threat not only to working class institutions but also to the welfare of society-at-large. Labour still wins the lion's share of the working class vote. There is no alternative party effectively competing for the working class constituency and therefore Labour is unlikely to be immediately replaced. Labour's problem in its working class constituency is one of morale and enthusiasm rather than competition, persuading its supporters to actually vote. The Labour vote may be securely anchored when compared with that of the Conservatives, but this is an essentially relative verdict. The fact remains that many blue-collar workers feel little loyalty to 'their' party and are aware of a lack of fit between the Labour Party's policies and their own aspirations. There are growing signs of Labour's supporters becoming willing to act outside the peaceful framework that the Party provides, as many were during the rent strike in progress at the time of Moorhouse and Chamberlain's research.[15] Although they were protesting against Conservative policies, by their actions as well as the views expressed in interviews, the rent strikers were also demonstrating their uncertainty that the Labour Party would prove a reliable and effective ally.

The situation we are describing is not simply one in which the Labour Party and trade union leaders are failing to adopt the 'right' policies which would unite the working class and reflect its aspirations. Our argument is rather that there exists a deeper and less easily resolved problem. Within the blue-collar strata, fragmentary currents allow contradictory values to co-exist. Members expect their trade union leaders to deliver the goods in the form of job security and pay increases, yet are suspicious of trade union power. Voters support Labour because it 'represents the working class' and expect to be appropriately rewarded, but simultaneously are often hostile to policies such as extending public ownership that might enhance working class interests. Media-type treatment analysing each successive issue that creates contention can conceal the broader problem—that it is doubtful whether any one monolithic labour movement can continue adequately to represent the working class. In the meantime, therefore, while not revolutionary, the condition of the working class remains volatile and unstable.

On account of their subordinate positions, dissent amongst blue-collar workers is always likely to be inflamed and therefore, the blue/white collar division must be considered a social cleavage of continuing importance. This traditional schism is not disappearing, but regarding it as the point in the class structure around which all threats to cohesion are focused and from which all critical pressures for social change are generated is becoming increasingly unrealistic. An equal challenge to cohesion now resides in the management of white-collar dissent. If the working class and the Labour movement are affected by developments in the class structure, we have been arguing that this applies at least equally to the middle classes and the Conservative Party that has acted as their political voice in the recent past. These are the political implications of the fragmentary class structure.

We have not reached the point where democracy is visibly collapsing, the people taking to the streets and the military intervening. If such a predicament had arrived there would be little need for social research to establish the facts. It is rather that a creeping decadence could eventually lead to political paralysis. On the surface all might seem well. Parliament meets and elections are held in which Conservative and Labour politicians continue to vie for public favour. There is a problem; a developing malaise in which the public's attachments to both parties are becoming tenuous, but as yet this is mostly beneath the surface and part of the country's predicament is that its political élites may not recognise the need to respond to the situation that has arisen. A succinct way of stating the problem is to view the emergent situation as one in which the political superstructure in Britain no longer reflects major grass-roots divisions of opinion and interest in society. Social change has undermined the foundations of existing political institutions, particularly the major parties. The superstructure has not toppled and will not break down overnight, but it is gradually ceasing to do its job effectively, this job being to articulate and compromise interests so as to produce an eventually acceptable framework within which social affairs can be transacted. At moments of relatively intense crisis such as February 1974, some observers have suggested that Britain is becoming ungovernable. As yet this is an overstatement, but it is certainly arguable that the political superstructure is no longer up to the job.

During its lifetime the 1966–70 Labour government lost electoral sympathy on a scale unprecedented in British post-war politics. In 1969 nothing seemed more certain than its defeat in the eventual general election. In 1970, however, only a last-minute swing in public opinion surprised the pollsters and returned a Conservative government. Our investigation was planned after these events and was designed to seek explanations of the electorate's volatility. However, the enquiry preceded the short-lived post-1970 Liberal revival, which was not predicted by anyone of consequence outside the Liberal Party itself, the collapse of the Heath administration, and the struggles of the subsequent Labour government to control inflation by implementing a voluntary social contract. The fieldwork for the investigation was completed in 1972 and the results cannot be legitimately used to interpret later events, though they offer obvious insights.

Political developments are not wholly determined at the level of grass-roots changes in the class structure and associated shifts in the public's attitudes. The ideological and organisational skills of political élites can make an independent contribution to the formation of political history. In themselves, therefore, the general fragmentary currents in the class structure that we have described may determine nothing, but if democratic political processes survive, these trends will favour the future success of political movements that are ideologically and organisationally looser coalitions than have dominated British politics in the recent past. This development will be necessary if the viewpoints now prevalent amongst different white and blue-collar sections of the fragmented public are to be effectively represented in the political process, and this is the condition for maintaining the confidence upon which a liberal democracy depends. The necessary changes could occur either within or at the expense of the presently dominant political parties. Their internal politics will decide this, and by their actions or inactivity they may hasten or delay the process, but they cannot avoid its necessity.

References

Chapter One—Introduction

1. Warner W. L. *et al.* (1957).
2. Coates K. and Silburn R. (1970).
3. Bott E. (1957).
4. Parkin F. (1971).
5. Ossowski S. (1963).
6. Lockwood D. (1966).
7. Parkin F. (1971).
8. Davies A. F. (1967).
9. Hiller P. (1975a and b).
10. Giddens A. (1973).
11. Wesolowski S. (1969).
12. Ossowski S. (1963).
13. Weinberg A. and Lyons F. (1972).

Chapter Two—White and blue-collar

1. For an acknowledgement and defence of this 'obsession' see the Introduction by D. V. Glass in Douglas J. W. B. (1964).
2. Such as Centers R. (1949) and Runciman W. G. (1966).
3. See Webb D. (1973). Note, however, that the data presented in Runciman W. G. (1966) appear inconsistent with Webb's findings.
4. Goyder J. C. (1975).
5. Wrong D. (1972).
6. Gorer G. (1971).
7. Bain G. S. (1972).
8. For evidence see Runciman W. G. (1966).
9. See Katona G. *et al.* (1971).
10. Sturmthal A. (1967).
11. See, for example, Runciman W. G. (1966).
12. Lockwood D. (1958).
13. Tropp A. (1957).
14. For data on long-term trends over time see Routh G. (1965).

15. Wynn M. (1972).
16. Evidence supporting this view can be found in Goldthorpe J. H. *et al.* (1969).
17. Mann M. (1973a).
18. See Lockwood D. (1958).
19. See Roberts B. C. *et al.* (1972).
20. Dale J. R. (1962).
21. Wedderburn D. (1970).
22. Bell C. (1968).
23. Bain G. S. and Price R. (1972).

Chapter Three—The embourgeoisement thesis and its critics

1. Zweig F. (1961); Turner G. (1963).
2. Westley M. A. and Westley M. W. (1972).
3. *Ibid.* See also Millar R. (1966).
4. Abrams M. (1960).
5. Willmott P. and Young M. (1960); Berger B. (1968).
6. Goldthorpe J. H. *et al.* (1969).
7. Lockwood D. (1966).
8. Bott E. (1957).
9. Popitz H. *et al.* (1969).
10. As respectively described in *The Dockworker*, Liverpool University Press (1954); Dennis N. *et al.* (1956); Tunstall J. (1962).
11. Cannon I. C. (1967).
12. Hoggart R. (1957).
13. As described in Young M. and Willmott P. (1957) and Kerr M. (1958).
14. These conclusions are argued in detail in Goldthorpe J. H. (1970).
15. Lockwood D. (1966).
16. Mackenzie G. (1973).
17. Mackenzie R. and Silver A. (1968).
18. Nordlinger E. A. (1967).
19. See Jessop B. (1974), Foster J. (1974) and Moorhouse H. F. (1973).
20. Carter I. (1974).
21. Newby H. (1975).
22. Batstone E. (1972).
23. Stacey M. *et al.* (1975) p. 121.
24. Platt J. (1971).
25. This view is developed in Parkin F. (1971) and also in Moore R. (1974).
26. Parkin F. (1967).
27. Ineichen B. (1972).
28. Mackenzie G. (1973) p. ix.
29. See Coleman T. (1965); Gray R. Q. (1974).
30. Foster J. (1968).

31. Clayre A. (1974).
32. For relevant descriptive material see Moore R. (1974).
33. For example see Young M. and Willmott P. (1957).
34. Blauner R. (1964).
35. Chivers T. S. (1973).

Chapter Four—Working class mobility orientations and education

1. Central Advisory Council for Education (1954 and 1959); Committee on Higher Education (1963).
2. Little A. and Westergaard J. (1964).
3. Noble T. (1974).
4. See Halsey A. H. (1972) and Ford J. (1969).
5. For an account of these theories see Bernstein B. (1971).
6. Bernstein B. (1971). See also Gahagan D. M. and Gahagan G. A. (1970) and Cook Gumperz J. (1973).
7. Rosen H. (1972); Heber M. (1974); Pap M. and Csaba P. (1974); Wootton A. J. (1974).
8. Labov W. (1973).
9. Jackson B. and Marsden D. (1962).
10. For a detailed portrait of middle class attitudes towards education see Seeley J. R. *et al.* (1956).
11. Mays J. B. (1962).
12. Young M. and McGeeney P. (1968).
13. Central Advisory Council for Education (1967).
14. Bott E. (1957).
15. Lockwood D. (1966). Subsequent investigators have sometimes treated any sign of ambition amongst working class families as evidence of embourgeoisement. For instance, see Toomey D. M. (1969).
16. These implications are spelt out in Lane M. (1972).
17. Banks O. and Finlayson D. (1973).
18. Boudon R. (1973).
19. Empey L. T. (1956).
20. Turner R. H. (1964).
21. Empey L. T. (1956); Stephenson R. M. (1957).
22. Wan Sang Han (1969).
23. Caro F. G. and Philblad C. T. (1964–5).
24. Himmelweit H. T. *et al.* (1952).
25. Boudon R. (1973). Other contributors to this line of argument include Jencks C. *et al.* (1973) and Milner M. (1972).
26. Krauss I. H. (1964).
27. Turner R. H. (1964).
28. Wilenski H. L. and Edwards H. (1959); Turner R. J. and Wagenfeld M. O. (1967).

29. See Miliband R. (1969) and Parkin F. (1971).
30. Hopper E. (1971).

Chapter Five — A class for itself?

1. For recent examples see Blackburn R. and Cockburn A. (1967).
2. See Glyn A. and Sutcliffe B. (1972).
3. Westergaard J. and Resler H. (1975). p. 52.
4. *Ibid.*, p. 17.
5. *Ibid.*, p. 343.
6. *Ibid.*, p. 200.
7. Popitz H. *et al.* (1969).
8. For an example and a very lucid discussion of factory consciousness see Beynon H. (1973).
9. Variants of this argument are employed by Miliband R. (1969), Parkin F. (1971), Mann M. (1973b) and Jessop B. (1974).
10. See Cohen S. and Young J. (1973).
11. Moorhouse H. F. (1973).
12. Foster J. (1974).
13. Michels R. (1959).
14. Parkin F. (1971).
15. Mann M. (1972).
16. Parkin F. (1971).
17. Mann M. (1970).
18. Moorhouse H. F. and Chamberlain C. W. (1974) and Chamberlain C. W. and Moorhouse H. F. (1974).
19. See Lane T. and Roberts K. (1971).
20. Brown R. K. and Brannen P. (1970); Brown R. K. *et al.* (1972).
21. Cousins J. (1972).
22. Mann M. (1972).
23. *Ibid.*

Chapter Six — The modern organisation and the new middle class

1. Webb D. (1973).
2. Lewis R. and Maude A. U. E. (1949).
3. Bonham J. (1954).
4. Runciman W. G. (1966).
5. Roberts B. C. *et al.* (1972).
6. Whyte W. H. (1956).
7. Mills C. Wright (1953).
8. Riesman D. *et al.* (1950).
9. Merton R. K. (1968b).

10. Vogel E. (1963).
11. Reich C. A. (1970).
12. Bechhofer F. *et al.* (1974 a and b).
13. Bell C. (1968).
14. Kohn M. L. (1971).
15. Crozier M. (1971).
16. Lansbury R. (1974).
17. Pahl J. M. and Pahl R. E. (1971).
18. Birch S. and Macmillan B. (1972).

Chapter Seven—The white-collar proletariat

1. Bain G. S. (1970); Bain G. S. and Price R. (1972b).
2. Goldthorpe J. H. *et al.* (1969).
3. An early statement of this argument appears in Strauss G. (1954).
4. Cook F. G. (1972).
5. Sykes A. J. M. (1964); Burns R. K. (1956).
6. Mercer D. E. and Weir D. T. H. (1972).
7. Roberts B. C. *et al.* (1972).
8. Blain A. J. N. (1972).
9. Blackburn R. M. (1967).
10. Prandy K. (1965).
11. Sturmthal A. (1967).
12. Bain G. S. *et al.* (1973).
13. McCarthy W. E. J. and Parker S. R. (1968).
14. Bain G. S. (1970).
15. Wrong D. (1972).
16. Neale R. S. (1972).
17. Mackenzie G. (1973).

Chapter Eight—The new radicals

1. Barker P. and Spence N. (1975).
2. For an example, see Chamberlain C. W. and Moorhouse H. F. (1974).
3. See Lipset S. M. and Altbach P. G. (1967); Kahn R. M. and Bowers W. J. (1970).
4. This view is expounded by Althusser L. (1971).
5. Hoch P. and Schoenbach V. (1969); Kidd H. (1969); Blackstone T. *et al.* (1970).
6. Feuer L. (1969).
7. Wilson B. (1970).
8. Gusfield J. (1970).
9. This criticism is also developed by Salter B. (1973).

10. Examples of this school of thought include Roszak T. (1970) and Reich C. A. (1970).
11. Reich C. A. (1970).
12. See Lipset S. M. and Altbach P. G. (1967) and Kahn R. M. and Bowers W. J. (1970).
13. Blackstone T. *et al.* (1970).
14. Lipset S. M. and Altbach P. G. (1967).
15. Halsey A. H. and Trow M. (1971).
16. See Lipset S. M. and Ladd E. C. (1971).
17. Mannheim K. (1936).
18. For example see Lipset S. M. (1960).
19. O'Boyle L. (1970).
20. Flacks R. (1970 and 1972).
21. Kohn M. L. (1971).
22. Parkin F. (1968).
23. Newton K. (1969).
24. Hindess B. (1971).

Chapter Nine—Politics in the fragmentary class structure

1. Dahrendorf R. (1968).
2. For a persuasive and influential statement of this theory see Lipset S. M. (1960).
3. Husbands C. T. (1975).
4. Barker P. and Spence N. (1975).
5. Butler D. and Stokes D. (1969).
6. *Ibid.*; Cotgrove S. and Vamplew C. (1972); Seabrook J. (1971).
7. Castles S. and Kosack C. (1973).
8. Butler D. and Stokes D. (1969).
9. Webb D. (1973).
10. For example see Westergaard J. H. (1972).
11. This point of view is argued in Dahrendorf R. (1959), Bell D. (1960) and Ross A. M. and Hartman P. T. (1960).
12. See Panitch L. (1976).
13. See Hindess B. (1971).
14. Barker P. and Spence N. (1975).
15. Moorhouse H. F. and Chamberlain C. W. (1974); Chamberlain C. W. and Moorhouse H. F. (1974).

Bibliography

Abrams M. *et al. Must Labour Lose?* Penguin, Harmondsworth, 1960.

Althusser L. *Lenin, Philosophy and other essays*, New Left Books, London, 1971.

Bain G. S. *The Growth of White-Collar Trade Unionism*, Clarendon Press, Oxford, 1970.

Bain G. S. *et al. Social Stratification and Trade Unionism*, Heinemann, London, 1973.

Bain G. S. and Price R. 'Who is a white-collar employee?', *British Journal of Industrial Relations*, 10, 1972(a), pp. 325–39.

Bain G. S. and Price R. 'Union growth and employment trends in the United Kingdom 1964–1970', *British Journal of Industrial Relations*, 10, 1972(b), pp. 336–81.

Banks O. and Finlayson D. *Success and Failure in the Secondary School*, Methuen, London, 1973.

Barker P. and Spence N. 'People and power', *New Society*, 29 May and 5 June 1975.

Batstone E. V. 'Organisational size and class imagery', paper presented to SSRC conference on *The Occupational Community of the Traditional Worker*, Durham, 1972.

Bechhofer F. *et al.* (a). 'Small shopkeepers: matter of meaning and money', *Sociological Review*, 22, 1974, pp. 465–82.

Bechhofer F. *et al.* (b). 'The petits bourgeois in the structure', in Parkin F. (ed.), *The Social Analysis of Class Structure*, Tavistock, London, 1974.

Bell C. *Middle Class Families*, Routledge, London, 1968.

Bell C. and Newby H. 'Sources of variation in agricultural workers' images of society', paper presented to SSRC conference on *The Occupational Community of the Traditional Worker*, Durham, 1972.

Bell D. *The End of Ideology*, Free Press, New York, 1960.

Berger B. *Working Class Suburb*, University of California Press, Berkeley, 1968.

Bernstein B. *Class Codes and Control*, Vols 1, 2 and 3, Routledge, London, 1971.

Beynon H. *Working for Ford*, Penguin, Harmondsworth, 1973.

Birch S. and Macmillan B. 'Managers on the move', *New Society*, 4 May 1972.

Blackburn R. M. *Union Character and Social Class*, Batsford, London, 1967.

Blackburn R. and Cockburn A. (eds.). *The Incompatibles*, Penguin, Harmondsworth, 1967.

Blackstone T. *et al. Students in Conflict: L.S.E. in 1967*, Weidenfeld and Nicolson, London, 1970.

Blain A. J. N. *Pilots and Management*, Allen and Unwin, London, 1972.

Blau P. M. 'Social mobility and interpersonal relations', *American Sociological Review*, 21, 1956, pp. 290–5.

Blau P. M. and Duncan O. D. *The American Occupational Structure*, Wiley, New York, 1967.

Blauner R. *Alienation and Freedom*, University of Chicago Press, 1964.

Bonham J. *The Middle Class Vote*, Faber, London, 1954.

Bott E. *Family and Social Network*, Tavistock, London, 1957.

Boudon R. *Education, Opportunity and Social Inequality*, Wiley, New York, 1973.

Brown R. K. and Brannen P. 'Social relations and social perspectives amongst shipbuilding workers: a preliminary statement', *Sociology*, 4, 1970, pp. 71–84 and 197–211.

Brown R. K. *et al.* 'The contours of solidarity: social stratification and industrial relations in shipbuilding', *British Journal of Industrial Relations*, 10, 1972, pp. 12–41.

Bulmer M. *Working Class Images of Society*, Routledge, London, 1976.

Burns R. K. 'Unionisation of the white-collar worker', in Shister J. (ed.), *Readings in Labour Economics and Industrial Relations*, Lippincott, Chicago, 1956.

Butler D. and Stokes D. *Political Change in Britain*, Macmillan, London, 1969.

Cannon I. C. 'Ideology and occupational community: a study of compositors', *Sociology*, 1, 1967, pp. 165–85.

Caro F. G. and Philblad C. T. 'Aspirations and expectations', *Sociology and Social Research*, 49, 1964–5, pp. 465–74.

Carter I. 'Agricultural workers in the class structure: a critical note', *Sociological Review*, 22, 1974, pp. 271–9.

Castle S. and Kosack G. *Immigrant Workers and the Class Structure in Western Europe*, Oxford University, London, 1973.

Centers R. *The Psychology of Social Classes*, Princeton University, New Jersey, 1949.

Central Advisory Council for Education. *Early Leaving*, HMSO, London, 1954.

Central Advisory Council for Education. *15–18* (Crowther Report), HMSO, London, 1959.

Central Advisory Council for Education. *Children and their Primary Schools* (Plowden Report), HMSO, London, 1967.

Chamberlain C. W. and Moorhouse H. F. 'Lower class attitudes towards the British political system', *Sociological Review*, 22, 1974, pp. 503–25.

Chivers T. S. 'The proletarianisation of a service worker', *Sociological Review*, 21, 1973, pp. 633–56.

Clayre A. *Work and Play*, Weidenfeld and Nicolson, London, 1974.

Coates K. and Silburn R. *Poverty: the forgotten Englishmen*, Penguin, Harmondsworth, 1970.

Cohen S. and Young J. *The Manufacture of News*, Constable, London, 1973.

Coleman T. *The Railway Navvies*, Hutchinson, London, 1965.

Committee on Higher Education. *Higher Education* (Robbins Report), HMSO, London, 1963.

Cook F. G. *The Concept of Ideology and its application to the study of Trade Unions*, MA thesis, University of Liverpool, 1972.

Cook Gumperz J. *Social Control and Socialisation*, Routledge, London, 1973.

Cotgrove S. and Vamplew C. 'Technology, class and politics: a study of process workers', *Sociology*, 6, 1972, pp. 169–85.

Cousins J. 'The non-militant shop steward', *New Society*, 2 Feb. 1972.

Cousins J. and Brown R. K. 'Patterns of paradox: shipbuilding workers' images of society', paper presented to SSRC conference on the *Occupational Community of the Traditional Worker*, Durham, 1972.

Crozier M. *The World of the Office Worker*, University of Chicago Press, 1971.

Dahrendorf R. *Class and Class Conflict in Industrial Society*, Routledge, London, 1959.

Dahrendorf R. 'On the origin of inequality among men', in *Essays on the Theory of Society*, Stanford University Press, 1968.

Dale J. R. *The Clerk in Industry*, Liverpool University Press, 1962.

Davies A. F. *Images of Class*, Sydney University Press, 1967.

Davies R. L. and Cousins J. M. 'The "new working class" and the old', paper presented to SSRC conference on the *Occupational Community of the Traditional Worker*, Durham, 1972.

Dennis N. *et al. Coal is our Life*, Eyre and Spottiswoode, London, 1956.

Douglas J. W. B. *The Home and the School*, MacGibbon and Kee, London, 1964.

Elias N. and Scotson J. L. *The Established and the Outsiders*, Cass, London, 1965.

Empey L. T. 'Social class and occupational aspiration', *American Sociological Review*, 21, 1956, pp. 703–9.

Feuer L. *The Conflict of Generations*, Heinemann, London, 1969.

Flacks R. 'Social and cultural meanings of student revolt', *Social Problems*, 17, 1970, pp. 340–57.

Flacks R. 'Young intelligentsia in revolt' in Wrong D. H. and Gracey H. L. (eds.), *Readings in Introductory Sociology*, Macmillan, New York, 1972.

Ford J. *Social Class and the Comprehensive School*, Routledge, London, 1969.

Foster J. 'Nineteenth century towns—a class dimension', in Dyos H. J. (ed.), *The Study of Urban History*, Edward Arnold, London, 1968.

Foster J. *Class Struggle and the Industrial Revolution*, Weidenfeld and Nicolson, London, 1974.

Gahagan D. M. and G. A. *Talk Reform*, Routledge, London, 1970.

Giddens A. *The Class Structure of the Advanced Societies*, Hutchinson, London, 1973.

Glyn A. and Sutcliffe B. *British Capitalism, Workers and the Profits Squeeze*, Penguin, Harmondsworth, 1972.

Goldthorpe J. H. 'Images of class amongst affluent manual workers', *Review Française de Sociologie*, 11, 1970, pp. 311–38.

Goldthorpe J. H. *et al. The Affluent Worker in the Class Structure*, Cambridge University Press, London, 1969.

Gorer G. *Sex and Marriage in England Today*, Nelson, London, 1971.

Gouldner A. W. 'Cosmopolitan and local', *Administrative Science Quarterly*, 2, 1959, pp. 281–306.

Gouldner A. W. *The Coming Crisis of Western Sociology*, Basic Books, New York, 1970.

Goyder J. C. 'A note on the declining relationships between objective and subjective class measures', *British Journal of Sociology*, 26, 1975, pp. 102–9.

Gray R. Q. 'The labour aristocracy in the Victorian class structure', in Parkin F. (ed.), *The Social Analysis of Class Structure*, Tavistock, London, 1974.

Gusfield J. 'Beyond Berkeley', in Becker H. S. (ed.), *Campus Power Struggle*, Aldine, USA, 1970.

Hall J. and Jones D. C. 'Social grading of occupations', *British Journal of Sociology*, 1, 1950, pp. 31–55.

Halsey A. H. *Educational Priority*, HMSO, London, 1972.

Halsey A. H. and Trow M. *The British Academics*, Faber, London, 1971.

Heber M. 'A comparative study of the questions asked by two groups of seven-year-old boys differing in social class', *Sociology*, 8, 1974, pp. 246–65.

Hiller P. 'Social reality and social stratification', *Sociological Review*, 21, 1973, pp. 77–99.

Hiller P. 'The nature and social location of everyday conceptions of class', *Sociology*, 9, 1975(a), pp. 1–28.

Hiller P. 'Continuities and variations in everyday conceptual components of class', *Sociology*, 9, 1975(b), pp. 255–87.

Himmelweit H. T., Halsey A. H. and Oppenheim A. N. 'Some views of adolescents on some aspects of the social class structure', *British Journal of Sociology*, 3, 1952, pp. 148–72.

Hindess B. *The Decline of Working Class Politics in Britain*, MacGibbon and Kee, London, 1971.

Hoch P. and Schoenbach V. *LSE: The Natives are Restless*, Sheed and Ward, London, 1969.

Hoggart R. *The Uses of Literacy*, Chatto and Windus, London, 1957.

Hopper E. 'Educational systems and selected consequences of patterns of mobility and non-mobility in industrial societies', in Hopper E. (ed.), *Readings in the Theory of Educational Systems*, Hutchinson, London, 1971.

Husbands C. T. 'The National Front: a response to crisis', *New Society*, 15 May 1975.

Ineichen B. 'Home-ownership and manual workers' life-styles', *Sociological Review*, 20, 1972, pp. 391–412.

Jackson B. and Marsden D. *Education and the Working Class*, Routledge, London, 1962.

Jencks C. *et al. Inequality*, Allen Lane, London, 1973.

Jessop B. *Traditionalism, Conservatism and British Political Culture*, Allen and Unwin, London, 1974.

Kahn R. M. and Bowers W. J. 'The social context of the rank and file student activist', *Sociology of Education*, 43, 1970, pp. 38–55.

Katona G. *et al. Aspirations and Affluence*, McGraw-Hill, New York, 1971.

Keddie N. (ed.). *Tinker, Tailor ... The Myth of cultural deprivation*, Penguin, Harmondsworth, 1973.

Kelvin R. P. 'What sort of income policy?', *New Society*, 6 April 1967.

Kerr, M. *The People of Ship Street*, Routledge, London, 1958.

Kidd H. *The Trouble at LSE 1966–67*, Oxford University Press, London, 1969.

Kohn M. L. 'Bureaucratic Man: a portrait and an interpretation', *American Sociological Review*, 36, 1971, pp. 461–74.

Krauss I. H. 'Sources of educational aspirations among working class youth', *American Sociological Review*, 29, 1964, pp. 867–79.

Labov W. 'The logic of non-standard English', in Keddie N. (ed.), *Tinker, Tailor ... the myth of cultural deprivation*, Penguin, Harmondsworth, 1973.

Lane M. 'Explaining educational choice', *Sociology*, 6, 1972, pp. 255–66.

Lane T. and Roberts K. *Strike at Pilkingtons*, Fontana, London, 1971.

Lansbury R. 'Careers, work and leisure among the new professionals', *Sociological Review*, 22, 1974, pp. 385–400.

Lewis R. and Maude A. U. E. *The English Middle Classes*, Phoenix House, London, 1949.

Lipset S. M. *Political Man*, Doubleday, New York, 1960.

Lipset S. M. and Altbach P. G. 'Student politics and higher education in the United States', in Lipset S. M. (ed.), *Student Politics*, Basic Books, New York, 1967.

Lipset S. M. and Ladd E. C. 'College generations and their politics', *New Society*, 7 Oct. 1971.

Little A. and Westergaard J. 'The trend of class differentials in educational opportunity in England and Wales', *British Journal of Sociology*, 15, 1964, pp. 301–16.

Liverpool University Press. *The Dockworker*, 1954.

Lockwood D. *The Blackcoated Worker*, Allen and Unwin, London, 1958.

Lockwood D. 'Sources of variation in working class images of society', *Sociological Review*, 14, 1966, pp. 249–67.

Lynch H. 'Doctors' pay and the public', *New Society*, 25 Aug. 1966.

McCarthy W. E. J. and Parker S. R. *Shop Stewards and Workshop Relations*,

Royal Commission on Trade Unions and Employers Associations, Research Papers, 10, HMSO, London, 1968.

Mackenzie G. *The Aristocracy of Labour*, Cambridge University Press, London, 1973.

Mackenzie R. and Silver A. *Angels in Marble*, Heinemann, London, 1968.

Mann M. 'The social cohesion of liberal democracy', *American Sociological Review*, 35, 1970, pp. 423–39.

Mann, M. 'The ideologies of non-skilled industrial workers', paper presented to SSRC conference on the *Occupational Community of the Traditional Worker*, Durham, 1972.

Mann M. *Workers on the Move*, Cambridge University Press, London, 1973(a).

Mann M. *Consciousness and Action in the Western Working Class*, Macmillan, London, 1973(b).

Mannheim K. *Ideology and Utopia*, Kegan Paul, London, 1936.

Mays J. B. *Education and the Urban Child*, Liverpool University Press, 1962.

Mercer D. E. and Weir D. T. H. 'Attitudes to work and trade unionism amongst white-collar workers', *Industrial Relations Journal*, 3, 1972, pp. 49–60.

Merton R. K. 'Cosmopolitans and locals', in *Social Theory and Social Structure*, Free Press, New York, 1968(a).

Merton R. K. 'Bureaucratic structure and personality', in *Social Theory and Social Structure*, op. cit., 1968(b).

Michels R. *Political Parties*, Dover Publications, New York, 1959.

Midwinter E. *Priority Education*, Penguin, Harmondsworth, 1972.

Miliband R. *The State in Capitalist Society*, Weidenfeld and Nicolson, London, 1969.

Millar R. *The New Classes*, Longman, London, 1966.

Mills C. Wright. *White-collar: the American Middle Classes*, Oxford University Press, New York, 1953.

Milner M. *The Illusion of Equality*, Jossey-Bass, San Francisco, 1972.

Moore, R. *Pitmen, Preachers and Politics*, Cambridge University Press, London, 1974.

Moorhouse H. F. 'The political incorporation of the British working class', *Sociology*, 7, 1973, pp. 341–59.

Moorhouse H. F. and Chamberlain C. W. 'Lower class attitudes to property', *Sociology*, 8, 1974, pp. 387–405.

Neale R. S. *Class and Ideology in the Nineteenth Century*, Routledge, London, 1972.

Newby H. 'Deference and the agricultural worker', *Sociological Review*, 23, 1975, pp. 51–60.

Newton K. *The Sociology of British Communism*, Allen Lane, London, 1969.

Noble T. 'Intergenerational mobility in Britain', *Sociology*, 8, 1974, pp. 475–83.

Nordlinger E. A. *The Working Class Tories*, MacGibbon and Kee, London, 1967.

O'Boyle L. 'The problem of an excess of educated men in Western Europe 1800–1850', *Journal of Modern History*, 42, 1970, pp. 471–95.

Ossowski S. *Class Structure in the Social Consciousness*, Routledge, London, 1963.

Pahl J. M. and Pahl R. E. *Managers and their Wives*, Allen Lane, London, 1971.

Panitch L. *Social Democracy and Industrial Militancy*, Cambridge University Press, London, 1976.

Pap M. and Csaba P. 'Social class differences in the speech of six-year-old Hungarian children', *Sociology*, 8, 1974, pp. 267–75.

Parkin F. 'Working class conservatism: a theory of political deviance', *British Journal of Sociology*, 18, 1967, pp. 278–90.

Parkin F. *Middle Class Radicalism*, Manchester University Press, 1968.

Parkin F. *Class Inequality and Political Order*, MacGibbon and Kee, London, 1971.

Parkin F. (ed.). *The Social Analysis of Class Structure*, Tavistock, London, 1974.

Parsler R. 'Some social aspects of embourgeoisement in Australia', *Sociology*, 5, 1971, pp. 95–112.

Payne S. 'Typologies of middle class mobility', *Sociology*, 7, 1973, pp. 417–28.

Peters R. (ed.). *Perspectives on Plowden*, Routledge, London, 1969.

Platt J. 'Variations to answers to different questions on perceptions of class', *Sociological Review*, 19, 1971, pp. 409–19.

Popitz H. *et al.* 'The worker's image of society', in Burns T. (ed.), *Industrial Man*, Penguin, Harmondsworth, 1969.

Prandy K. *Professional Employees*, Faber, London, 1965.

Reich C. A. *The Greening of America*, Random House, New York, 1970.

Riesman D. *et al. The Lonely Crowd*, Yale University Press, New Haven, 1950.

Riessman F. *The Culturally Deprived Child*, Harper and Row, New York, 1962.

Roberts B. C. *et al. Reluctant Militants*, Heinemann, London, 1972.

Rosen H. *Language and Class*, Falling Wall Press, Bristol, 1972.

Ross A. M. and Hartman P. T. *Changing Patterns of Industrial Conflict*, Wiley, New York, 1960.

Roszak T. *The Making of a Counter-Culture*, Faber, London, 1970.

Routh G. *Occupations and Pay in Great Britain 1906–1960*. Cambridge University Press, London, 1965.

Runciman W. G. *Relative Deprivation and Social Justice*, Routledge, London, 1966.

Salter B. 'Explanations of student unrest: an exercise in devaluation', *British Journal of Sociology*, 24, 1973, pp. 329–40.

Seabrook J. *City Close-Up*, Allen Lane, London, 1971.

Seeley J. R. *et al. Crestwood Heights*, Constable, London, 1956.

Sexton P. C. and Sexton B. *Blue-collars and Hard Hats*, Random House, New York, 1971.

Stacey M. *et al. Power, Persistence and Change,* Routledge, London, 1975.
Stephenson R. M. 'Mobility orientation and stratification of 1000 ninth graders', *American Sociological Review,* 22, 1957, pp. 204–12.
Strauss G. 'White-collar unions are different', *Harvard Business Review,* Sept.–Oct. 1954, pp. 73–82.
Sturmthal A. *White-collar Trade Unions,* University of Illinois Press, 1967.
Sykes A. J. M. 'The problem of clerical trade unions: a review', *Scientific Business,* Aug. 1964, pp. 176–83.
Titmuss R. M. *Income Distribution and Social Change,* Allen and Unwin, London, 1962.
Toomey D. M. 'Home-centred working class parents' attitudes towards their sons' education and careers', *Sociology,* 3, 1969, pp. 299–320.
Tropp A. *The School-teachers,* Heinemann, London, 1957.
Tunstall J. *The Fishermen,* MacGibbon and Kee, London, 1962.
Turner G. *The Car-Makers,* Eyre and Spottiswoode, London, 1963.
Turner R. H. *The Social Context of Ambition,* Chandler, San Francisco, 1964.
Turner R. J. and Wagenfeld M. O. 'Occupational mobility and schizophrenia', *American Sociological Review,* 32, 1967, pp. 104–13.
Vogel E. *Japan's New Middle Class,* University of California Press, Berkeley, 1963.
Wan Sang Han. 'Two conflicting themes: common values versus class differential values', *American Sociological Review,* 34, 1969, pp. 679–90.
Warner W. L. *et al. Social Class in America,* Peter Smith, Mass., 1957.
Watson W. 'Social mobility and social class in industrial communities', in Gluckman M. (ed.), *Closed Systems and Open Minds,* Oliver and Boyd, Edinburgh, 1964.
Webb D. 'Some reservations on the use of self-rated class', *Sociological Review,* 21, 1973, pp. 321–30.
Wedderburn D. 'Workplace inequality', *New Society,* 9 Apr. 1970.
Weinberg A. and Lyons F. 'Class theory and practice', *British Journal of Sociology,* 23, 1972, pp. 51–65.
Wesolowski S. 'The notions of strata and class in socialist society', in Béteille A. (ed.), *Social Inequality,* Penguin, Harmondsworth, 1969.
Westergaard J. H. 'Sociology: the myth of classlessness', in Blackburn R. (ed.), *Ideology in Social Science,* Fontana, London, 1972.
Westergaard J. and Resler H. *Class in a Capitalist Society,* Heinemann, London, 1975.
Westley M. A. and Westley M. W. *The Emerging Worker,* McGill–Queens University Press, Montreal, 1972.
Whyte W. H. *The Organisation Man,* Simon and Schuster, New York, 1956.
Wilenski H. L. and Edwards H. 'The skidder', *American Sociological Review,* 24, 1959, pp. 215–31.
Willmott P. and Young M. *Family and Class in a London Suburb,* Routledge, London, 1960.
Wilson B. *The Youth Culture and the Universities,* Faber, London, 1970.
Witkin R. W. 'Social class influences on the amount and type of positive evaluation of school lessons', *Sociology,* 5, 1971, pp. 169–89.

Wootton A. J. 'Talk in the homes of young children', *Sociology*, 8, 1974, pp. 277–95.
Wrong D. H. 'Social inequality without social stratification', in Wrong D. H. and Gracey H. L. (eds.), *Readings in Introductory Sociology*, Macmillan, New York, 1972.
Wynn M. *Family Policy*, Penguin, Harmondsworth, 1972.
Young M. and McGeeney P. *Learning Begins at Home*, Routledge, London, 1968.
Young M. and Willmott P. 'Social grading by manual workers', *British Journal of Sociology*, 7, 1956, pp. 337–45.
Young M. and Willmott P. *Family and Kinship in East London*, Routledge, London, 1957.
Zweig F. *The Worker in an Affluent Society*, Heinemann, London, 1961.

Name Index

Subject Index